SIX FISH LIMIT

Books by Steve Raymond

Fly Fishing—Nonfiction
Kamloops: An Angler's Study of the Kamloops Trout
The Year of the Angler
The Year of the Trout
Backcasts: A History of the Washington Fly Fishing Club,
1939–1989
Steelhead Country
The Estuary Flyfisher
Rivers of the Heart
Blue Upright
Nervous Water: Variations on a Theme of Fly Fishing

Fly Fishing—Fiction
Trout Quintet: Five Stories of Life, Liberty and the Pursuit of Fly Fishing
Six Fish Limit: Stories from the Far Side of Fly Fishing

Civil War History
In the Very Thickest of the Fight: The Civil War Experience of the 78th
Illinois Volunteer Infantry Regiment

SIX FISH LIMIT

Stories from the Far Side of Fly Fishing

Steve Raymond

Skyhorse Publishing

Skyhorse Publishing books may be purchased in bulk at special discounts for sales promotion, corporate gifts, fund-raising, or educational purposes. Special editions can also be created to specifications. For details, contact the Special Sales Department, Skyhorse Publishing, 307 West 36th Street, 11th Floor, New York, NY 10018 or info@skyhorsepublishing.com.

Skyhorse® and Skyhorse Publishing® are registered trademarks of Skyhorse Publishing, Inc.®, a Delaware corporation.

Visit our website at www.skyhorsepublishing.com.

10 9 8 7 6 5 4 3 2 1

Library of Congress Cataloging-in-Publication Data is available on file.

Cover design by Kai Texel
Cover and interior art by Al Hassall

Print ISBN: 978-1-5107-7001-0
Ebook ISBN: 978-1-5107-7174-1

Printed in the United States of America

Credits
Two stories in this book were published previously.
"The Bonefisherman's Dilemma" first appeared in somewhat different form as "The $5,081 Misunderstanding" in *Gray's Sporting Journal*, vol. 29, no. 7, 2005.
"The First Words Ever Written about Fly Fishing" first appeared in *Fly Fisherman* magazine, vol. 47, no. 3, 2016.

For Joan, forever

CONTENTS

PREFACE

ARNOLD GINGRICH, late editor and publisher of *Esquire* magazine, once observed that fly fishers and symphony orchestra conductors have extra-long lives because they get so much upper-body cardio-vascular exercise waving fly rods or batons. Now that I have reached an age that proves the truth of his assertion, I've also discovered it has a downside: Long-lived fly fishers eventually reach a point of such decrepitude they can't fish much anymore, if at all.

Being unable to fish is bad enough, but for someone who writes about fly fishing, as I do, it's even worse; it means I no longer have a ready source of new nonfiction material. When that happens, there's only one thing left to do, and that's start writing fly-fishing fiction. I've done that once already in *Trout Quintet,* a collection of offbeat but mostly upbeat fly-fishing stories. This book, however, is a little different; it's perhaps a little more offbeat and a little less upbeat, more about some of the things that go on in what I call the far side of fly fishing—things that don't usually get into books.

Fly fishers, it seems, have always considered themselves an elite group, consigning those who fish by any other means to a hopeless pro-letariat. There's some justification for that feeling because fly fishing undoubtedly places greater physical and intellectual demands on its participants than any other type of angling, but that doesn't necessarily make fly fishers any more pure in heart than the rest of humanity. There are, I regret to say, some professed fly fishers who have forgotten the cautionary advice of Dame Juliana Berners that the sport is not for making or increasing your money, but rather for your physical and spiritual health. Those who ignore this advice often do so because they have succumbed to the temptation to use fly fishing for other reasons, usually personal gain. Others use it for self-aggrandizement, trying to build reputations they couldn't achieve any other way. Still others start with the most unselfish of motives only to run afoul of the law of unintended consequences. You'll meet all types in these pages and learn some of the strange, funny, and sometimes tragic things that happen to them. Let me add hurriedly, however, that all these stories are strictly fictional and the characters, places and situations they describe are all figments of my fish-filled imagination.

There. That should keep the lawyers happy.

The first character you'll meet here, in "The Bonefisherman's Dilemma," is Freddie Woodson, who planned to write a story about his visit to the Sugar Cay Bonefish Resort, sell it to a fly-fishing magazine and use the income to pay some of the trip expenses. But he didn't count on drinking too much rum, falling asleep in a hot tub, meeting a cute native girl, or losing the only bonefish he managed to hook. Now he's engaged in an increasingly acrimonious debate with his accountant: Freddie thinks the trip expenses should be deductible from his income tax even though the trip produced no income; his accountant disagrees. Just when a rupture appears inevitable, Freddie comes up with an ingenious but legally questionable way of deriving some income from the trip. Don't try this on *your* tax return.

"Welcome to the Stub Mountain Fly Shop," the next tale, introduces Vicki Brightman, who just inherited a financially struggling fly shop from her father. Realizing the shop is now her only means of support, she begins a desperate search for ways to rebuild the business, deciding finally that what works for fish—catching them with artificial flies—might just as easily work for fishermen. With that in mind she cooks up a wild scheme that even she thinks is crazy, but in the absence of a better idea she goes ahead with it—and it succeeds beyond her wildest dreams. Just so long as she doesn't dream about ethics.

This is followed by "The Fishlexic," a much shorter story featuring Dr. Timothy Hardhorn, an internationally prominent geneticist who also happens to be a fanatic fly fisher. Having just won a Nobel prize and married a glamorous supermodel, it seems Dr. Hardhorn could hardly desire anything more, but he still dreams of having a son who will grow up to become his lifelong fly-fishing companion. Since he's a geneticist, it's only natural that when his wife becomes pregnant Dr. Hardhorn decides to rearrange the embryonic genes to assure his son will grow up to be a fly fisherman. When young Rodney Hardhorn is born, his father's wish at first appears fulfilled, but as the boy grows older Dr. Hardhorn begins to notice a few things about his son that don't seem, well, quite normal. Finally he concludes that, thanks to his genetic manipulation, Rodney has an unusual form of dyslexia; he thinks every fish he catches is much larger than it really is.

Genetic manipulation: something you shouldn't try at home.

Next up is "Diary of an Unknown Angler." Here we meet Andrew Royster, a college professor who teaches classes in fly-fishing history and literature and owns a small bookshop specializing in classic fishing books. When he discovers an old diary that appears to hold the solution to one of fly fishing's greatest mysteries, Royster is more than delighted; he sees a chance to secure his own immortal place in the annals of fly-fishing literature by publishing the discovery, only to learn something he should have known all along—that after history is made and literature is written, it's very difficult to change either.

"The Man in Black Waders" started out short but eventually grew into a full-fledged novella. Here you'll meet Clint Steele, the most famous fly fisher in the world, as seen by an ambitious young reporter assigned to cover Steele's trial. The famous angler is being sued by Mickey Cutter, a retired teacher and author of a single obscure fishing book, who alleges Steele plagiarized his work. For Steele, the stakes couldn't be higher—he could lose not only lots of money but also his well-cultivated reputation, his livelihood, perhaps even his chosen way of life. When the jury returns its verdict, Steele does something entirely unexpected that appears to confirm the jury got it right.

The final tale is the whimsical, tongue-in-cheek "real" story of the first words ever written about fly fishing. Those words—*"I have heard of a Macedonian way of catching fish and it is this"*—are attributed to the Roman scribe Claudius Aelianus. But where did he hear them? Well, where else but at a meeting of his local fishing club? OK, so that's probably not the way it really happened, but who knows? Maybe it was. In any case, the first words ever written about fly fishing also are the last words written in this book.

I hope you enjoy reading these stories. I certainly enjoyed writing them, although I'd rather have been out fishing.

—Steve Raymond

THE BONEFISHERMAN'S DILEMMA

From: f.woodson@rightnowmail.com
To: andrea@brinkeraccounting.com
Subj: Sugar Cay trip expenses
March 19

Hi Andi—

Thanks for your email about the business expenses claimed on my income tax return for the trip to Sugar Cay Bonefish Resort. It reminded me why I'm so fortunate to have you as my accountant. I know you'll check everything thoroughly and I won't have a thing to worry about with the IRS.

Anyway, the expenses break down this way:

Five days guided fishing, six nights lodging: $3,750.00	
Guide's tip:	$150.00
Round-trip air fare:	$1,181.00
Total:	$5,081.00

I didn't claim expenses for the flies I bought for the trip because I might use them again and, unlike some people I know, I never fudge on my taxes! You wouldn't let me get away with it anyway.

I trust this answers the question in your email. Let me know if you need any further information.

Warmest regards,
Freddie

From: f.woodson@rightnowmail.com
To: andrea@brinkeraccounting.com
Subj: Sugar Cay trip expenses
March 26

Dear Andi:

What do you mean I can't claim the Sugar Cay Bonefish Resort trip as a business expense? As you know, I'm paid to write fishing stories for outdoor magazines. I have to travel to various fishing destinations to gather material, and that costs money. I'm sure you've heard the old expression that sometimes it's necessary to spend money in order to make money; well, that's how it is with us outdoor writers.

Actually, there are a lot of guys who do this, and I'd appreciate it if you wouldn't nose that around; the competition is tough enough already.

The IRS also might get suspicious if it received too many claims for fishing trips as business expenses.

In my case, however, there's no doubt the trip to Sugar Cay was a legitimate business expense. There's no other way I could have gotten material for a story.

I trust this will put your doubts to rest.

Cordially,
Fred

From: f.woodson@rightnowmail.com
To: andrea@brinkeraccounting.com
Subj: Sugar Cay trip expenses
March 30

Dear Andrea:

I have your most recent email. In response to your question about where the Sugar Cay bonefish story was published and how much I was paid for it, the answer is that there was no story. The truth is I didn't catch a single bonefish.

Sometimes things just turn out that way: You travel a long way to fish and either the fish don't cooperate or the weather is miserable or something else goes wrong. But that's one of the charms of fishing; you never know what's going to happen.

I know some "outdoor writers" who think nothing of making up lurid fish-filled stories even if they don't catch anything, but I would never do that because I consider it unethical. I'm sure you feel the same way. Nevertheless, the Sugar Cay trip is a legitimate business expense because it was undertaken as part of my work and certainly *would* have resulted in a story if I had caught any fish.

Sincerely,
Frederick

From: f.woodson@rightnowmail.com
To: andrea@brinkeraccounting.com
Subj: Sugar Cay trip expenses
April 4

Dear Ms. Brinker:

Here it is less than two weeks before filing deadline and I can't believe we're still quibbling over the expenses for the Sugar Cay trip! Frankly, I doubt the necessity of the request in your last email for a full explanation of why the trip did not result in an income-producing story. I can't imagine why either you or the IRS needs to know that. It makes me wonder if I made the right decision hiring you as my accountant.

Nevertheless, in the interests of settling this matter in the time remaining before the April 15 filing deadline, I have decided, albeit reluctantly, to comply with your request. Here is a full account of what happened at Sugar Cay:

Monday: After checking in, I met my guide, Nelson, and we headed out on the flats to look for bonefish. Do you have any idea how hard it is to see a bonefish? It's tough under any circumstances, but on this particular day the wind was blowing, the surface was choppy, and we couldn't see anything. Nelson is an expert at spotting bonefish, but even he admitted it was impossible. After several hours we gave up.

Tuesday: I woke up with a killer headache and an upset stomach. Possibly it was due to the local water, or maybe the three rum punches (or was it four?) I had before bed. I can't believe it was the rum punches, though; they were s-o-o-o-o good. Anyway, feeling as wretched as I did, I told Nelson to take the day off.

Wednesday: I got up early, raring to go, then fell asleep in the hot tub. By the time I woke up, Nelson had gone home, so I couldn't fish. But the day wasn't wasted; I took a walk into the village and met a cute little native girl named Sallie.

Thursday: Nelson pounded on my door at 5:30 a.m. but before I could say anything Sallie hollered at him to get lost. There was nothing else to do but stay in bed.

However, I'm sure you'll appreciate the fact that I didn't claim an expense for the necklace I bought Sallie.

Friday: I met Nelson early in the morning and we headed for the flats. Conditions were perfect. We hadn't been wading long when Nelson pointed and said, "Bonefish, mon, 2 o'clock." I thought my cast was right on target, but the fly disappeared in a big swirl of mud and Nelson told me the fish had spooked. We resumed searching and Nelson spotted several other good-sized bonefish, but they all spooked when I cast. Finally, Nelson said, "Dis time, mon, try to lead de fish a little."

The next fish we saw was a real whopper, maybe the biggest bonefish I've ever seen. I remembered what Nelson had said and dropped the fly a few feet in front of the fish. "Strip, strip!" Nelson whispered, then "Stop!" I stopped. "Now strip again!" I resumed stripping and felt resistance. The bonefish was on! It ran like its tail was on fire, peeling line off my reel at an unbelievable rate. Boy, was I excited!

Then suddenly the line went slack; the fish was gone. I reeled in and discovered one of my leader knots had failed. I suppose it wasn't a very good idea to start tying leaders after all those rum punches. Oh, well, live and learn.

We didn't see any more bonefish after that, so that's why there was no story. I trust this explanation will satisfy both you and the IRS.

Yours very truly,
Frederick Woodson

From: f.woodson@rightnowmail.com
To: andrea@brinkeraccounting.com
Subj: Sugar Cay trip expenses
April 11

Ms. Brinker:

I strongly disagree with your conclusion that in the absence of an income-producing story of the trip, the costs of the Sugar Cay expedition cannot be claimed as a business expense on my income tax return. However, the question is irrelevant because now I can declare some income resulting from the trip.

After reviewing our correspondence relating to this dispute, I decided to submit the whole works to an outdoor magazine for publication. It was accepted and the magazine has just sent me a check for $600.

In the sincere hope that this will get both you and the IRS off my back, I remain

Disgruntledly yours,
Frederick N. Woodson, Esq.

WELCOME TO THE STUB MOUNTAIN FLY SHOP

IT WAS well past 11 p.m. when the last person left, an old, drunk fisherman who bumped into the door frame on his way out. Vicki Brightman sighed with relief as she watched him stagger away. It had been the longest evening of her life.

She'd thought having a wake for her father would be a good idea, a nice party for his fishing and fly-tying friends and customers at the Stub Mountain Fly Shop. She invited everyone to come at 4 p.m., but two hours later she was beginning to think she'd made a huge mistake. The crowd was by far the largest ever to jam into the shop. Nearly all were men; the few women who showed up departed hurriedly after extending brief condolences. By the time the last old fisherman stumbled out the door, they had drained a full keg of beer, offered innumerable slurred toasts to her dad, Curly Brightman, and suffered through what seemed like dozens of maudlin speeches and teary reminiscences.

It had been a helluva party, that was for sure, and Curly probably would have enjoyed it had he been able to attend. But now she was the only person left in the shop, and as she looked around she saw it

7

was a shambles. A lot of beer had been spilled on the floor along with empty paper cups, fractured remains of potato chips, clots of dip, fragments of bread, meatballs, cheese and cold cuts, all mingled in an ugly slush. The smell of spilled beer even overwhelmed the perpetual fly-shop odor of mothballs. Some of the plastic trays filled with flies were covered with breadcrumbs and potato-chip fragments and several dry flies were floating on top of the spilled beer. Vicki suspected at least a few flies had also departed in the pockets of celebrants, along with a couple of bottles of dry-fly dope, packets of feathers, boxes of hooks, and God only knew what else.

And she was left alone to clean it all up.

But that, she decided, could wait until morning. Heaving another deep sigh, she went to the counter, took out a marking pen and made a sign that said, "Shop Closed Until Further Notice." She taped the sign to the front door, locked the door, pulled the shades over the windows, then let herself out the back, locked the back door and trudged uphill to the old frame house in the woods behind the shop. It was the house where she had spent all forty-two years of her life with her dad. She could barely remember her mother, who had been taken by cancer when Vicki was only seven years old. Now, with Curly gone, too, it seemed like the house was empty of spirit.

She climbed the steps to her second-floor room, washed her face where several celebrants had planted beery kisses, undressed quickly, pulled on a nightshirt, and tumbled into bed. Exhausted as she was, she expected to fall asleep quickly.

But she didn't. As had happened so often in the nights since Curly passed away, her mind seized on the frightening realization that she was now sole owner and proprietor of the Stub Mountain Fly Shop, her only means of support. That was the scariest part; she'd known for years the shop's business was declining. Her father had patiently taught her to tie flies when she was barely into her teens until she got to be at least as good as he was—and he had been very good indeed. Then he asked her to start taking turns behind the counter or helping customers when he was otherwise occupied, and she learned the location of everything in the inventory and mastered the fly-fishing jargon of the shop's customers.

So it was easy for her to see the business start going downhill.

The shop's location had once seemed ideal. It stood right next to Route 206, the last stop before the Powder Horn National Forest and its wealth of fly-fishing waters—Glint Lake, the Powder Horn River, Buck River, Te-Hoosh Creek, Misty Lake, and the five fertile lakes of the Stairstep Chain. Anglers headed that way stopped at the shop to buy licenses, and once inside they almost invariably remembered something else they needed—leader material, mosquito repellant, maybe a new fly line, certainly some flies—and all those purchases added to the shop's bottom line, making it financially healthy for years.

Then the number of drop-in visitors slowly but surely began declining. Partly it was because the state went to an online system for ordering fishing licenses, which meant anglers didn't have to stop at the Stub Mountain shop to get them anymore. Partly it was because the sons of many of the shop's old customers stayed home playing video games instead of going fishing with their dads. And much of it was because competing shops marketed their wares aggressively through printed or online catalogs, which meant anglers could conveniently stay at home, order anything they needed, and have it shipped right away.

As Vicki witnessed the shop's business decline, she tried everything she could think of to help her father keep it afloat. When he started trying to sell stuff online—which meant hiring a spectacled geek to set up and maintain a website—she pitched in to handle orders, pack merchandise, and take it to the post office. Sometimes that kept her away from helping customers or tending the inventory, and Curly finally decided to throw in the towel on the Internet venture.

Next, he tried running guided trips from the shop, but most anglers who fished the Powder Horn waters didn't think they needed guides, and most of the guides proved unreliable anyway. Liability insurance also was so expensive that the venture quickly lost money, and Curly shut it down. Then he started placing small advertisements in fly-fishing magazines—they had to be small because anything larger cost too much—but when the ads brought no discernible increase in business, he stopped doing that, too. An experiment with an online newsletter brought the same results. He put big signs in the shop windows advertising sales with bargain prices on rods, reels and other merchandise, even a "happy hour" deal on flies, but that didn't work, either.

His next idea was to bring in a couple of big-name fly-fishing celebrities to put on advertised "clinics" at the shop, but few people showed up and the costs vastly exceeded the modest revenues. He even considered bulldozing a pond and stocking it with trout, but the cost of permits, construction, hatchery trout, and food to keep them alive seemed prohibitive, with little prospect of being offset by revenues. There was also the small matter of the lack of a running water source to keep the pond oxygenated and the trout alive, and he abandoned that idea, too.

So nothing worked, and for the past several months, even though fishing in the national forest was reported fabulous, the little bell that rang over the door when a customer entered the shop remained silent for hours at a time, and Vicki could see her father growing ever more concerned about the shop's viability. Now she couldn't help wondering if those worries had led to the terrible morning eight days ago when she found him cold and unresponsive in his bed.

Vicki kept a private list of things she would never think about. One was Roger, a guy she thought she loved, but they broke up when he told her she always smelled of mothballs. Well, she wouldn't think about Roger. Bait fishermen also were high on her list. So was her real name. She hadn't even shared it with Roger, let alone anyone else.

Only Vicki and her father knew her real name was Vixen. She'd been given that name because she was born with red hair, reminding her father of the classic fly pattern known as the Hendrickson, as dressed by the great fly tyer Art Flick, who used the urine-stained hair of a female red fox, or vixen, to make the fly's body. By the time Vicki was five years old, however, her mother's genes had asserted themselves and her hair had turned dark and straight; she'd been a long-haired brunette ever since. It was also at age five when she decided she wanted to be called Vicki. After all, what girl ever would want to be called Vixen?

Another thing on her list of things not to think about was the downward spiral of her father's business. But now it was her business, and she would have to think about it.

She'd gone through the shop's books—something he'd never permitted her to do—and discovered things were in even worse shape than she'd thought. To keep the shop afloat her father had been burning through what little money he'd managed to save over the years, and now there wasn't much left. If the shop was going to survive, she would have to think of something drastic to save it.

Of course, she could try to sell the shop and the home behind it, but given present economic circumstances the shop would never fetch a decent price, and the old house probably wouldn't, either. Besides, both had been the anchors of her life, and she wasn't yet prepared to think of parting with them. Even if she did, what would she do then? At age forty-two, she was still single and had no desire to be otherwise. Her only serious romance had been with Roger, whom she would not think about. She had no wish to go through that again.

So her sleepless thoughts ended up where they always did: If she wanted the shop to provide even a modest living, she would have to find a way to keep it afloat.

She spent the next two days scrubbing, mopping, wiping, vacuuming, and dusting. She emptied each of dozens of little compartments containing flies, removed crumbs and potato-chip fragments from the compartments and put the flies back, except those too badly damaged by beer or other spills. She neatly rearranged all the packets of fly-tying materials, all the spools of tying silk, floss and tinsel; all the packages of hooks, tools, fly dope and leader material; all the magazines, books and videos and countless other items. But all the while she worked, her mind also was working, trying to come up with an idea to stimulate the business. She mentally inspected each notion, ultimately discarding it and going on to another. By day's end she was thoroughly exhausted, but her mind kept busy all night, and she got little sleep.

When daylight flooded her room, she felt as if she had a bad hangover. For a long while she stayed in bed and tried to coax herself to sleep, but it was useless. Her rebellious brain kept reminding her she needed to find a way to make the shop solvent, because that was the only way *she* could remain solvent.

Giving up on sleep, she crawled out of bed and tried to revive herself with a shower, then went through the motions of eating a late breakfast or early lunch; she wasn't sure which. She decided to spend what remained of the day prowling the Internet in search of ideas, since she hadn't been able to come up with any good ones herself.

She started by looking at the websites of competitors, beginning with the largest, Keegan's Compleat Fly Shop, which had become a rapidly growing force in the fly-fishing business. Years ago Vicki had gone with her father to the annual Fly Tackle Dealers Show in Denver where she met Jeff Keegan, the dynamic young owner of the company. At the time he'd owned only one fly shop, but now he had three—Manhattan, Denver, and Seattle—plus a huge mail-order catalog and Internet business, selling virtually anything fly fishers or fly tyers could want. Rumor had it that his rapid expansion was fueled with family money, which Vicki believed was probably true because she didn't think anybody ever got rich in the fly-fishing business. She remembered Jeff as an attractive guy, about her age, and maybe a good catch, especially if the rumors of family money were true. But that was while she was tangled up with Roger, who she wouldn't think about, and the possibilities, if that's what they were, slipped away.

Now she scrolled through Keegan's website with growing dismay. It had a variety and quantity of merchandise several times greater than the little Stub Mountain Fly Shop, plus a wide choice of trips to exotic fly-fishing destinations all over the world, a busy schedule of fly-fishing, fly-tying, and rod-building schools and camps, and a large menu of private pay-to-play waters for its customers to fish. Its selection of flies, tackle, and accessories positively dwarfed the meager inventory of Vicki's shop. How could she possibly compete with such a Goliath?

Looking at the website merely depressed her, so she started searching those of smaller retailers. That depressed her even further, because they also were much bigger than the Stub Mountain Fly Shop, so she switched her search to fly-fishing blogs and forums, sifting through inane postings of misspelled words and butchered grammar that convinced her the American system of public education had badly failed its students, at least those who were fly fishers.

What was left? She thought of the big stacks of old fly-fishing magazines and catalogs in her father's office and spent the afternoon leafing through them, hoping some useful thought or idea would leap out at her. She came across articles and advertisements for float tubes and pontoon boats, reminding her of the lemminglike stampede of stillwater fly fishers to buy those things when they came on the market. They sold like crazy; she remembered one month when they sold fourteen in the shop. She never understood why because she knew from experience they made fly fishing far more difficult than other fishing platforms, especially those that allowed anglers to stand up to see everything and pivot quickly to cast in any direction. Now the continued popularity of the boob tubes, as she called them, seemed as inexplicable as ever.

Not that it did her any good.

Finally she gave up, locked the shop, trudged uphill to the empty house, and made herself a ham sandwich for dinner. After that she watched television for a while, trying to divert her crowded thoughts, but found nothing worth watching. Giving up, she headed upstairs to her room, put on her nightshirt, and climbed into bed, even more exhausted than she'd been the previous night.

But sleep still wouldn't come. Her mind remained fixed on the problem of her future, which, no matter how she examined it, seemed inextricably tied to her old house and the fly shop. After hours of tossing and turning, she suddenly thought of one more possible source of ideas she hadn't explored: Her father's collection of fly-fishing books. That got her out of bed and downstairs to check the bookshelves in his den.

There were at least a couple of hundred books, most about fly patterns or fly tying. Some were relatively new but most were old, some even a lot older than Curly had been. They were arranged more or less in alphabetical order, so the first one she picked up was a well-thumbed copy of *Fly Patterns of Alaska*. Nothing there; at least, nothing that promised the salvation of a failing fly shop. But she continued searching, skimming pages in a vain canvass for ideas, until she came to *The Streamside Guide to Naturals and Their Imitations*, by Art Flick—the guy who inspired her father to give her the name she wouldn't think about. She skipped that one and went onto the next.

At length she came to a book that reminded her of another lemminglike stampede of fly fishers to buy what was then considered a revolutionary development—fly patterns without hackles. That was before her time, but she remembered reading about the flies and how her father told her that for a while it was impossible to keep no-hackle patterns in the shop they sold so fast. Yet she also recalled he said he never saw any evidence no-hackle patterns were any better than conventional flies, and their eventual near disappearance seemed to indicate he was right.

Nobody, she thought, ever accused fly fishers of being unsusceptible to advertising. But how did that help her?

By the time the first glimmer of daylight was visible outside, all she had for her efforts were a sore neck and eyes that kept trying to close even as she fought to keep them open. Then she suddenly realized she'd been holding the same book in her lap, open to the same page, for what must have been a long time. She put the book aside, stood stiffly, climbed back upstairs and went to bed. This time she fell asleep quickly.

When she awoke the light was low, and she thought it was still morning until she realized the light was coming from the opposite side of the house; she'd slept all day and now it was early evening. She still didn't feel refreshed, though; instead she felt as if she had a hangover, like the morning after the wake. Reluctantly, she crawled out of bed, made a breakfast-dinner of scrambled eggs, bacon, toast, and two cups of strong black coffee, and decided to devote what remained of the evening to continue searching Curly's books for a fly-shop-saving idea.

Which she did with furious resolve but no result until sometime, long after midnight, she came across something that struck her as . . . well, a little unusual. It wasn't a eureka moment, just a small thing she found in a thin, old, dusty book hidden between two bigger volumes, a book she'd never seen before. The title was *Field and River Sports*, written by someone named A. F. Cuthbert and published in Toronto in 1905. It was about bird hunting and fly fishing in British Columbia, and as she turned to the fly-fishing section, the book fell open to a page featuring a fly pattern called "Major Neely's Excellent Sedge."

There was no explanation of who Major Neely was, or how and where he fished his sedge, but she immediately noticed something odd about the dressing: The body was made of goose flank feathers dyed olive green, packed tightly together, then trimmed short to form a thin, cylindrical shape. The remainder of the pattern was conventional—a wing of mottled turkey feather plus several turns of furnace hackle on a size 7 or 9 hook. She knew the hook sizes were from an old, obsolete numbering system and it wasn't clear from the accompanying illustration that the body was made of goose feathers, but the result was still a good-looking imitation of an adult caddis fly, which she knew British Columbia anglers called a sedge.

As a veteran fly tyer, Vicki knew it would take plenty of goose feathers and lots of time to make a body like that. Who would do such a thing? And why, when it would be so much faster and easier to use wool or dubbing material? She was glad she'd never had to tie this fly, but the pattern was so unusual it stuck in her memory as she returned the old book to its place and went on with her search, and when she finally came to the last of her father's books—*Lee Wulff on Flies*—she still hadn't found anything that could conceivably help the Stub Mountain Fly Shop return to solvency; nothing like float tubes or no-hackle flies that would inspire fly fishers to reach for their wallets.

After another restless night, she awoke thinking of Major Neely's Excellent Sedge pattern, though she didn't know why. Maybe it was because the Excellent Sedge was the only thing that had caught her attention during her tedious search. But one thing she did know: Even though she still hadn't figured out how to make it profitable, she needed to reopen the shop. It had been closed several days, and she was losing at least a little income each day it remained shut, so she resigned herself to return to work. After breakfast she went to the shop, removed the "closed" sign from the door, and opened for business.

It was a long time before the bell over the door signaled the arrival of what she hoped was the day's first customer, a thin young man who entered and looked around as if he'd never been in a fly shop before, then approached the counter and nervously asked for directions.

Vicki gave them as affably as she could. He thanked her and said "nice shop" on the way out.

After that Vicki sat in lonely silence while she tried again to think how she could make a living from the "nice shop." When nothing came to mind, she decided she really needed to do something useful, like tie some flies. The table she and her father had used for tying was still set up next to the counter, so she sat in her dad's old chair and thought about which flies in the store's inventory of patterns needed replenishing. She hadn't looked, and now she didn't want to bother.

That's when she remembered Major Neely's Excellent Sedge. Why not tie one? Most of what she needed was already on the table, but she had to fetch a packet of goose flank feathers from the shop's stock. She couldn't find any dyed green goose feathers, so she decided to use natural gray instead. Soon she was cursing under her breath as she tried to secure feathers around the hook and pack them tightly together. Whoever Major Neely was, he must have been crazy, she thought. This was torture.

She was still sitting there, frowning at the mess on the hook, when the bell over the door sounded, and a middle-aged guy walked in with two little boys in his wake. She could see his wife outside waiting in a car. He told Vicki his family was trying to escape California for a few days and wanted to go fishing in the Powder Horn National Forest. While he spoke, the kids started racing through the shop, playing tag or something, hollering, knocking packaged fly-tying materials off their display pegs, and scattering flies from open compartments. Their father shouted at them to desist, but they were oblivious to his orders and kept roughhousing until their mother looked in and saw what was happening. She marched into the store like a drill sergeant, brought the kids up short, and herded them outside.

With the kids from hell removed, Vicki managed a cordial conversation with their father, who bought a couple of spools of leader material and a dozen flies on her recommendation. He thanked her and even helped her pick up the fallen packages of materials and loose flies the kids had left scattered on the floor.

Those awful kids. She remembered Roger had told her he wanted children. But she wouldn't think about Roger.

Anyway, the California customer left her with more than $40 in the till, her first cash transaction as owner of the Stub Mountain Fly Shop. That made her feel good.

Still feeling good, she returned to the unfinished fly in her vise and immediately grew frustrated as she resumed her struggle with the goose feathers. Why would anyone choose such feathers for body material? Then it occurred to her that in the early twentieth century, when Major Neely was presumably tying flies, British Columbia was probably a pretty wild, empty place without any shops where you could get dubbing, wool or other fly-tying materials. Maybe Neely, whoever he was, was forced to rely on indigenous materials. Maybe gray goose feathers were common in that time and place.

Gray goose feathers were still common, but white goose feathers were even more plentiful. They also were easy to dye in different colors, such as olive green, light brown, or even orange for October caddis patterns. Vicki had dyed lots of goose feathers for her dad, using cooking pots on the kitchen stove and spreading the dyed wet feathers on newspapers to dry. It was a messy business, not one she enjoyed, but she had gotten good enough at it to be able to produce dyed feathers in almost any color Curly needed.

Returning to the table, she went back to work and finally trained her fingers to the point where she was able to wrap the feathers around the hook shank and pack them together fairly easily. What she ended up with was a body that looked a little like a bottle brush, with goose flank feathers sticking out from the hook in all directions, but that was easily fixed with a sharp pair of scissors. She trimmed the feathers closely on all sides, leaving a hefty pile of severed fibers on the fly-tying table. The trimming left the fly with a thin, dark gray cylindrical body that looked just like the illustration in the old book.

She took the fly out of the vise and ran her fingers over the body. It felt like some sort of soft fur. Anyone looking at it would never guess what material had been used to make it.

Hmmm. That, she thought, was interesting.

She put the unfinished fly back in the vise, chose a single feather of genetically modified blue dun gamecock for the hackle, and substituted dark brown deer hair for the turkey wing of the original, leaving a little topknot of hair just behind the eye of the hook to add buoyancy to the fly. The finished product looked good. She thought it would look even better with a green or brown body.

But so what? A new fly pattern, particularly an untested pattern, wasn't going to help the Stub Mountain Fly Shop get back on its feet.

Or was it?

She didn't see how. But it had been a pretty good day; she had finally solved her frustrations with the Excellent Sedge, made her first sale as master of the shop, and ended up with more than $40 in the till. All in all, the best day since Curly's passing.

That night she slept at least a few hours only to wake in darkness with her mind in a whirl. A kaleidoscope of thoughts and images flashed through her consciousness—the wreckage inside the shop after Curly's wake, Keegan's Compleat Fly Shop website with its huge inventory, her canvass of fly-fishing blogs and forums; the tedious search of Curly's magazines and books, the landslide popularity of float tubes and no-hackle flies, kids from hell running through the shop, Curly insisting no-hackle flies were no better than any others, and on and on until finally, sometime in the gray, fuzzy hours of early morning, some of the pieces started to fit together and the germ of an idea began taking root in her brain. Yet even as she conceived it, it seemed impossibly outrageous and improbable, one of those thoughts that seem clever in the middle of the night but utterly foolish by the harsh light of day.

She decided she'd think about it later and went back to sleep.

Her alarm clock startled her awake at 7 a.m. It was the first time she'd set the alarm since Curly passed away, but today would be another day of business at the Stub Mountain Fly Shop. At least she hoped so.

She was up, showered, dressed, and fixing breakfast when last night's crazy idea came back to mind. She tried to examine it mentally, viewing it from all angles, each time concluding that it was impossible and the odds against success insurmountable.

Yet what else did she have? If she did nothing, she might be able to hang on for a while, but business undoubtedly would continue declining, and the shop's value would decline with it until eventually she would be forced to sell for much less than she thought it was really worth. Then what would she do?

The thought was so troubling it distracted her until she became aware of the smell of burning bacon. She turned off the stove, let the blackened bacon cool, tossed it in the garbage, and started over, this time paying attention to what was happening in the frying pan. But when she finally sat down to eat her toast and bacon, her mind again began wrestling with the night-time idea that seemed to have lost all its glitter by day.

This time, however, she tried to consider it from another angle: What did she have to lose by trying it? Things couldn't be any worse than they were already. And if she tried it, at least she'd have the feeling she was doing *something* to try to rescue the shop, even if she had little confidence that what she was doing could succeed.

She finished her breakfast and decided to take a walk in the woods behind the house, mulling over her nascent scheme. She loved the forest, its fresh scent and the way the foliage filtered sunlight so it fell in bright spatters on the forest floor. She also loved the feel of moss underfoot and the songs of kinglets, wrens, and thrushes. Then she realized she was hearing an unfamiliar bird call, three high, crisp notes that her mind translated into three quick, insistent words: "Go for it, Go for it, Go for it." Was nature sending a message? That her crazy idea might be worth trying after all?

Maybe. With the persistent bird call ringing in her ears, she returned to the house and resumed her seat at the kitchen table, this time with paper and pen, and started making a list of everything she would have to do.

The first was to call Jimmy the Geek, the guy who'd set up the shop website; she had several things to ask him. Next was to call Peter Pomeroy, her dad's lawyer, and make an appointment to see him next Monday, in Fultonville, the nearest town, twenty-seven miles away. The shop was always closed Monday so she'd be free then. She'd already been in touch with Pomeroy about probating her father's estate, but now there was something else she needed him to do.

She'd also have to do some shopping in Fultonville. The shop was running low on mothballs, and she needed groceries, including some brownie mix.

Then she would have to call her suppliers and order lots of white goose flank feathers, more dry-fly hooks, and some olive, brown, orange, and black dye.

Finally, she had to telephone some of the women who contracted to tie flies for the shop. There were seven in all, but she would call only the five best tyers. She wouldn't call the shop's male contractor tyers; she didn't completely trust them because they were men.

After that, whenever she could find time, she had to face the messy job of dying lots of goose feathers. That was everything she could think of, and it seemed like a lot.

Two very busy weeks later everything was ready. She'd written the announcement and photo she wanted on the shop website, sent them to Jimmy the Geek, and he had them ready to post. He'd also set up the new email accounts she wanted him to register with the pseudonymous names she had given him. She'd met with Peter Pomeroy, told him what she wanted, and he'd prepared a nondisclosure agreement with convoluted legal language which, in plain English, said more or less that "if you breathe a word of this to anyone, I'll sue your pants off." She'd stocked up on mothballs, groceries, brownie mix, goose feathers, hooks, and dye. She'd dyed lots of feathers and tied lots of flies. She'd invited the five women contract fly tyers to a coffee klatch at the shop where she served brownies and told them most of what she was planning to do, demonstrated how to tie Major Neely's Excellent Sedge pattern, swore them to secrecy, and had each one sign the nondisclosure agreement.

But now it was Tuesday morning, the first day in the shop's business week. When Curly was alive, either he or Vicki would take Tuesdays off while the other one looked after the shop. That way one of them could have two days off in a row every other week to go fishing or do whatever else he or she wanted. Now that it was just her alone, Vicki would have to work six-day weeks until she could find and train some trustworthy person to fill in for her—and figure out how to pay that person. She hoped it wouldn't be too long before she could do that.

Her first act before opening the shop was to call Jimmy the Geek and tell him to post the announcement on the website and the color photo to go with it. At this hour of the morning he sounded even more zoned out than usual, but he called back moments later to say the notice and the photo were up. Using the computer on the shop counter, she logged onto the website and read it:

> The Stub Mountain Fly Shop is proud to announce it has become exclusive purveyor of a revolutionary and highly effective new series of trout fly patterns called the Stub Mountain series. There are four patterns in the series, three adult caddis dry-fly imitations with a choice of olive, brown or orange bodies in hook sizes 8, 10, and 12, and a black chironomid pupa imitation in sizes 10, 12, or 14. The caddis

> patterns are priced at $3.95 each, the chironomids at $2.95 each. The flies will be sold through the shop or by email or telephone order (see the "contact" window of this website). Payment by credit card, check, or PayPal.
>
> Only finished flies will be sold. The patterns and materials are proprietary and remain the exclusive property of the Stub Mountain Fly Shop.

Her breath escaped as she finished reading; she hadn't realized how tense she'd been. Then she examined the color photo of the flies beneath the announcement; she'd taken the shot with her digital camera after carefully arranging the four patterns. She thought they looked good.

Now for the next step. Using one of the phony email names— "Weight Forward"—she logged onto the regional fly fisher's forum and posted a fictitious fishing report, reminding herself to throw in some misspellings or grammatical errors to make it seem real:

> Great fishing at Misty Lake over the weekend. Released forteen Rainbows up to 18½ inches on a olive-bodied caddis, one of the new flys for sale at the Stub Mountain Fly Shop. Check them out!

She read it over several times until she was satisfied, then sent it to the forum. She'd made her cast; now she hoped for a rise.

Her next task was to remove the shop's stock of expensive fly reels from the locked glass case bolted to the counter and place them on a high shelf. Then she filled the glass case with a display of sedges and chironomids tied by the women contract fly tyers. The chironomid patterns were simple, with thin, tapered bodies of trimmed dyed black goose flank feathers ribbed with fine silver wire. A sprig of white ostrich herl at the head simulated the gills of the natural. When the display was complete, she locked the case and placed a printed copy of the website announcement on top. Nobody would be able to get a close-up look at the flies without removing the announcement.

Now all she had to do was wait for customers.

The day passed slowly and quietly. Too slowly and too quietly. A phone call around 10 a.m. was a wrong number. There were no email messages. The bell over the door didn't ring, and not a single customer entered the shop. The sky outside was slate gray and threatening, which matched her mood. She tried to fill the time tying flies until she grew tired of that, then thumbed through the latest issue of *Tippets*, the current favorite magazine of fly fishers, but found little of interest. By the time she dejectedly closed the shop and trudged uphill to her house to microwave a frozen pizza, she was beginning to think her big idea was a bust.

The thought lingered in her troubled mind well into the evening until she finally went to the cupboard where Curly kept a bottle of his favorite bourbon. She poured herself a couple of stiff ones, which eventually helped her get to sleep. But next morning, when the alarm clock jarred her awake, she wondered if there was any point getting out of bed. The temptation to stay there was great, and she did for a while, but eventually she peeled off the blankets and got up, hurried through breakfast and headed for the shop, where she turned on the computer and anxiously checked for email messages.

There were none.

Next she checked the shop website to make sure the announcement was still there. It was.

Mentally she recited her vocabulary of obscenities, which was extensive thanks to her lifelong association with fishermen. That made her feel a little better, but not much.

Maybe it was time to try something else. She returned to the computer, logged onto Twitter and posted her first "tweet" as "Fly Dude":

Get your tail up to Stairstep Lake No. 4. Hot fishing for big browns on dry olive-bodied caddis, one of the new Stub Mountain series of flies. Check it out.

After that she settled down again to wait. She was just about to doze off behind the counter when the bell rang over the door. Hoping for a customer, she looked up quickly, then saw it was only Jimmy the Geek. His hair as usual was unkempt, the clothes on his skinny frame looked as if he'd slept in them, and his big thick glasses magnified the acne scars on his pale face. Awkward as usual in both speech and manner, he told Vicki he'd just stopped by to see if everything was OK with the website.

"Yeah, it's fine," she said. "The only problem is, nobody is looking at it."

With a little hemming and hawing, Jimmy allowed as how that was a problem beyond his ability to fix.

"I know that, but it was very kind of you to stop by. I really appreciate it." That was true; she hadn't realized how starved she was for contact with another human being, although she wasn't quite sure Jimmy fit the definition.

Apparently unable to think of anything else to say, Jimmy looked briefly around the shop, squeaked goodbye, and left, leaving Vicki wondering if the real reason he'd stopped by was because he was developing a crush on her. Oh Lord, spare me that, she thought.

The rest of the morning passed so slowly that when noon came she was surprised it was still Wednesday. She hadn't brought anything for lunch, so she locked the shop briefly, ran up the hill, fixed herself a peanut-butter sandwich, and ran back, wondering why she was hurrying since no customers were waiting when she returned.

Resuming station behind the counter, she ate the sandwich and, for lack of anything better to do, logged onto the Internet as "Leaky Waders" and composed another fictitious fishing report for the local fly-fishing forum:

Big caddis hatch on Te-Hoosh Creek yesterday. Lots of trout on size
12 dry brown caddis, one of the new flies available at the Stub Mountain Fly Shop. Let me tell you, guys, this is one grate fly!

Well, she thought, maybe that will bring them in, and sent the message.

But nobody came, the phone remained silent and there were no
emails. The afternoon passed slowly. At closing time she glumly
locked the shop, made her way back to the house, and this time went
directly to the bottle of bourbon and lowered its level considerably.
With nothing else on her stomach, and no desire to eat, she stumbled
upstairs, crawled in bed and fell asleep almost instantly. Sometime
later she awoke from a vivid dream that the shop was full of customers clamoring for her versions of Major Neely's Excellent Sedge,
only to realize the reality was that she was in bed with a headache and
was hungry. A dose of cheese on toast took care of the hunger and
after a while she managed to get back to sleep, and when the alarm
woke her in the morning her headache was gone.

But that was the only sign of encouragement the morning brought.
When she reopened the shop and checked for email messages there
were none, and there were no messages on the telephone answering
machine. A few cars passed on the highway but none stopped, and
no customers entered the store. It was so quiet she thought she could
hear dust particles falling to the floor, and as the morning dragged on
her frustration increased with each passing empty moment. Finally it
boiled over. "To hell with it!" she hollered, though there was no one
else to hear. She had to do something or go crazy.

But what? Without a real purpose in mind, she went to the computer, logged on, and began a digital blitz, using all the pseudonymous
names Jimmy the Geek had registered. She sent emails and tweets
to every destination she could think of, the local fly-fishing forum
and several others, to blogs and websites and every email address in
the lengthy directory Curly had built up over the years, which probably included a number of people who were dead. All the messages

described incredible catches on the new fly patterns available only from the Stub Mountain Fly Shop.

Not surprisingly, some of the emails bounced back immediately as undeliverable, but Vicki didn't care; even those were welcome since she hadn't had a message from anyone else.

When at last she ran out of addresses to send phony emails, she stopped, calmed down and began to assess what she'd just done. She had relieved her pent-up frustration, that much was clear, but had she overreacted? Screwed up everything? Shot herself in the foot? She wondered if maybe she had.

There was only one way to find out, and that was to wait and see what happened when all those emails began reaching their targets.

The first call came in a little after 11 a.m. A raspy male voice on the other end identified itself as belonging to Harley. "I saw your post on the web and I might want to buy some of your flies," he said, "but $3.95 is an awful lot for a fly. Are they guaranteed?"

Vicki wasn't sure she understood. "What did you say?"

"I asked if your flies are guaranteed."

"Guaranteed to do what?"

"Why, catch fish, of course."

"Uh, no, they're not guaranteed to catch fish. That part is up to you."

"Well, then, almost four bucks a fly is way too much. Thanks anyway." And Harley hung up.

"I can't believe this," Vicki said out loud.

"Whatsa matter?" someone answered. It was Jimmy the Geek; she hadn't heard him enter the shop while she was on the phone.

"After all that work and all the emails and tweets I sent out the first call I get is some guy who wants to know if the flies are guaranteed. Jeez!"

Jimmy looked like a scolded puppy. "Well," he said finally, "at least somebody saw one of your emails."

Vicki wasn't sure how to reply, or even if she wanted to, but then she noticed her computer was signaling she had an email. She clicked on the inbox and found the message, which was from somebody named Ed Hasbrouck: "Just saw your email about the new flies. I'd like to place an order for half a dozen of the olive-bodied caddis patterns in size 8." The remainder of the message included shipping details and billing information.

"Come look at this!" Vicki hollered.

Jimmy the Geek crowded in next to her, a little more closely than she thought was necessary. His breath smelled as if he'd brushed his teeth with garlic. He read the email and said "Awesome! First order. Wow!"

The phone rang again. It was another order, this time from a guy in Somerville, and he didn't ask for a guarantee. Five more orders came in the next hour, two by phone and three by email. Then a big SUV with Idaho license plates pulled up outside the shop. The driver stepped out, dressed as if he'd just finished posing for the L.L. Bean catalog. He walked into the shop, came directly to the counter and surveyed the locked display case containing the new flies.

"So these are the famous flies, huh?" he said. "They're all over the Internet, so I thought I'd better stop and see them for myself." He peered closely through the top of the glass at the display inside. "Good-looking flies," he said. "I'll take two of each pattern in each size."

Scarcely believing her ears, Vicki unlocked the case, removed the flies and placed them in one of the cheap, foam-lined plastic fly boxes Curly had ordered for just such purposes, thinking as she did that she might need to order more. Then she used a calculator to add up the order and was astonished at the total—$88.80, by far the largest sale she'd made since reopening the shop. Then the stranger said he also needed a new weight-forward six-weight fly line, which added $90 to the total. Vicki was almost giddy when he handed over his credit card and she ran it through the card reader on the counter.

The shop seemed quiet after he left until Vicki realized Jimmy was still there, lurking in the corner pretending to examine some fly-tying materials on display. It was after noon and she was getting hungry, but the way orders were coming in now she didn't think she could afford to leave, so she told Jimmy where to find the peanut butter and bread in her kitchen. "Awesome," he said, and went scurrying up to the house to get them.

He was barely out the door when the phone rang again. "Stub Mountain Fly Shop," she answered. An antagonistic male voice said, "Who the hell do you think you are, trying to keep your fly pattern secret? All I have to do is buy one and strip it down. Then I'll post the pattern all over the Internet."

"And I'll sue you for every miserable thing you've got," she said.

"Listen, you little . . . " but Vicki hung up before he could say anything more, then waited for a surge of adrenaline to pass. This was not what she'd expected when she went public with her flies; she wondered if she'd have to get used to it.

By the time Jimmy the Geek returned with two awkwardly made peanut-butter sandwiches wrapped in a napkin, Vicki had fielded three more email orders. With orders piling up rapidly, she realized she needed to figure out a standard procedure to handle each one. She'd also need to order more padded shipping envelopes and cheap plastic fly boxes and figure out a way to get completed orders to the post office in Fultonville. All would take time and/or money, cutting into profits, but she remembered the old saying that you have to spend money in order to make money. She decided she'd have to get used to that.

She took a bite from one of the sandwiches only to find that Jimmy had slathered about half an inch of peanut butter on the bread, which made her teeth stick together. She was still trying to clear away the excess peanut butter when the phone rang again. "Shtub Mounshan Fly Shob," she answered. It was another order, this one from a polite man who didn't call her any names or ask why she sounded so funny.

And so it went until it was time to close the shop and she had to tell Jimmy the Geek to go home.

Next morning there were fourteen more email orders on the computer and five on the telephone answering machine, and Vicki realized she was going to need help. She thought of calling Jimmy but decided that might give him the wrong idea. Instead, she called Anne Walling, one of the shop's contract fly tyers who lived nearby, to ask if she could come in for a while to keep an eye on things while Vicki dealt with the increasing pile of orders. Anne was an empty nester without much to do except tie flies and keep house for herself and her husband, and Vicki thought she might welcome a chance to get out of the house. She said she'd be at the shop in an hour.

Anne had spent enough time in the shop to have a good idea where things were and Vicki walked her through the procedure for using the credit-card machine and cash register, then sat down to deal with the pile of orders while Anne settled herself on Curly's old stool behind the counter. Vicki was making progress when she heard the bell ring over the door and looked up, expecting to see Anne's first walk-in customer; instead, it was Jimmy the Geek who entered. "Uh, I thought you might need some help," he told Vicki, glancing at Anne.

"Jimmy, this is Anne Walling," Vicki said. "She's helping me out today. Anne, this is Jimmy." Anne extended her hand, but Jimmy just looked at it with a puzzled expression on his face and said nothing; that's when Vicki realized he was even more socially inept than she'd thought. She was about to send him on his way when she had an idea; maybe Jimmy could help after all. She knew he drove an old, battered Volkswagen Beetle with a bicycle strapped on top which he called his "lifeboat."

"How'd you like to take a load of completed orders to the post office in Fultonville and mail them?" she asked. "And maybe get me some more padded shipping envelopes? I'll give you the money and pay for your time."

"Awesome," Jimmy said.

She handed him a stack of addressed shipping envelopes, took some money from the till, gave it to him, and told him to bring her the receipts. She knew sending him to Fultonville would keep him out of her hair at least a couple of hours, maybe longer. He had several customers in town—"clients," he called them—people who paid him to help manage their websites or solve computing problems. He took the money and packages eagerly and headed for the door.

"Nice to meet you," Anne called after him, but Jimmy said nothing as he departed.

"What's with him?" Anne asked.

"He's socially handicapped, a total geek. But he is kind of handy to have around now and then." From the look on her face, Vicki knew Anne doubted that.

Then the bell rang again and a customer walked in, went to the display case of flies on the counter and picked out a dozen. Three more drop-in customers came during the next hour, each buying flies and other items—leader material, fly dope, maps of the national forest, and a pair of cheap Polaroid sunglasses. While Anne handled their purchases, Vicki kept busy fielding orders over the phone or email.

Afternoon came almost before they knew it and Jimmy returned. He came with an armload of padded shipping envelopes and a couple of receipts and deposited them on the counter in front of Vicki, along with a handful of change. Then he went back outside and returned with a brown paper bag and handed it to her. "Uh, I brought you a present," he said, eyes downcast.

Vicki hefted the bag. It was heavy. She opened it and found an extra-large jar of peanut butter. "Oh, Jimmy, that was so thoughtful of you," she said, stifling laughter. She lifted the jar out of the bag. "And you got the creamy kind. That's great; I don't like the crunchy stuff."

Jimmy's face reddened, but he said nothing, just stood there until she realized he was waiting for her to pay him. She opened the till and removed a twenty-dollar bill. "Will this cover it?" she asked.

"Oh, that's too much. Way too much. You don't need to pay me anything. I was glad to help."

"That's not the way this works, Jimmy. You get paid for your time and your gas." She thrust the bill on him and he took it awkwardly, put it in his pocket and continued standing there, still not looking her in the eye. "Anything else I can do?" he asked finally.

"No thanks, Jimmy. I think we've got it under control."

"Oh. Well, OK then. I guess I'd better be going." He turned and shuffled toward the door.

"Thanks again for the peanut butter," she called after him.

"Sure." The bell rang and he was gone.

"Boy, does he ever have a crush on you," Anne said.

"No kidding. How could you tell?"

They both laughed. But Vicki couldn't help thinking that things with Jimmy were close to getting out of hand.

She turned back to the orders and was finally caught up by midafternoon when there was a lull. She took advantage of it to go online and check a couple of fly-fishing forums where earlier she had planted fictitious fishing reports. To her delight there were two new reports, apparently genuine. A guy who identified himself as "Fly Daddy" told of a delightful day on the Powder Horn, with more than a dozen good-sized trout caught and released on an olive sedge pattern from the Stub Mountain Fly Shop. "This is a great fly," he said. "Hustle over to the Stub Mountain Fly Shop and get some while they last."

Maybe I should hire him, Vicki thought.

Another post, this one from "Blood Knot," described an epic battle with a four-pound rainbow in one of the Stairstep Lakes, although he didn't specify which one. "Chironomids were hatching, the trout were rising and I covered a humongous rise and this big guy came up and took it, and what a fight! Oh, yeah, the fly was one of them new chironomid patterns from Stub Mountain Fly Shop. Good fly." It was the first mention she'd seen of anyone using the chironomid pattern and she was glad to see it; she expected the end of the seasonal caddis hatch eventually would lead to a decline in sales of those patterns, at least until it was time for the October caddis, but she was hoping sales of the chironomid pattern would fill the gap; she knew from her fishing experience that chironomids hatched from the beginning of the fishing season until the end.

Next she found a terse tweet from somebody named Jake: "Wednesday at Te-Hoosh Creek. Seventeen rainbow released on green caddis dry fly from Stub Mountain Fly Shop. Great pattern." Nice, she thought.

She was about to continue searching when another new email order came in and she went back to work, and when closing time came and she paid Anne out of the till, she was pleased to look back on the day as perhaps the best yet.

Saturday brought fewer email and phone orders but more drop-in customers, nearly all of whom bought some of the new flies. One also bought a pair of wading shoes, which raised his tab well above a hundred dollars. It was closing time before she realized the day had passed without a visit from Jimmy the Geek. Well, that was OK with Vicki.

Sunday was similar, with brisk business from drop-ins on their way to or from the fishing in the national forest. Once when she looked out, she thought she saw Jimmy's Volkswagen rattling past, but he didn't stop. Maybe he has a new girlfriend, she thought. Or hoped.

By Monday morning Vicki was thoroughly tired. The past week, while amazingly successful, had also been exhausting. She remained late in bed, finally got up, fixed brunch, and thought about the rest of the day. It was tempting just to do nothing, or maybe go fishing. Lord, how long had it been since she'd been fishing? But as she contemplated those choices, she had a nagging feeling that she needed to dye some more goose feathers to keep her contract fly tyers supplied, so she began that messy, tedious task.

Finished by midafternoon, she spread the newly dyed feathers on newspapers and left them to dry, then went to the shop to see how many orders might have come in overnight or in the morning. She didn't really want to do that, but after going to all the work and worry to establish this landslide of business she also felt an obligation to try to keep up with it, and keep her customers from having to wait for their orders just because she wanted to take a day off.

She let herself into the shop, went to the counter, and turned on the computer. While waiting for it to boot up, she checked the telephone answering machine: Three orders. She opened the order file on the computer and added those, then opened the email program and found eleven more orders. While she worked to fill those, four more came in, and by the time she'd finished packaging and addressing all eighteen orders it was late and she was getting hungry.

As she locked the shop and made the trek uphill, she decided she'd earned a little reward, so after cleaning up the dyed goose feathers she took a T-bone steak from the refrigerator, filled the grill in front of the house with charcoal, lit it, then made a salad and some garlic bread. While waiting for the coals to ripen, she opened a bottle of zinfandel—chef's prerogative—poured a glass and sipped while the steak was grilling. When all was ready, she enjoyed the best dinner she'd had in a long while.

After that she watched some depressing news on television, made a fruitless attempt to find something else worth watching, gave up, and devoted an hour to one of Nick Lyons' enjoyable fly-fishing books before crawling wearily into bed.

It was sometime after midnight when a sudden noise woke her. She lay still, listening, and it came again, a metallic scrape that seemed to come from outside. She got out of bed, opened the drawer in her bedside table and removed Curly's old .45-caliber automatic, checked to see it held a loaded magazine, picked up the flashlight she kept on the table, and started downstairs. Moving as quietly as possible, she went to the front door, softly turned the dead bolt, then opened the door partway and looked out.

A faint cone of light gleamed from inside the garbage can in back of the shop, disclosing a man bent over the can, rummaging around inside. She reached for the switch and turned on the outside lights, causing the man to straighten up in the sudden flood of illumination. He was well dressed, obviously not a tramp or homeless person. He blinked in the light, then turned and started running toward the highway where a shiny new SUV was parked on the roadside. He jumped in the driver's seat, started the engine, and drove away in a spray of gravel.

When he was gone, Vicki realized she was trembling. After taking several deep breaths, she made her way to the garbage can, still clutching the heavy pistol and flashlight. She thought she knew what the intruder had been looking for—something that might reveal the material used to make the bodies of the Stub Mountain flies—but she knew there was nothing in the can but miscellaneous scraps from dozens of fly patterns along with some discarded bubble pack and other refuse from the shop, plus a few orange peels. Using the flashlight, she saw fragments of bubble pack and a couple of orange peels scattered around the can; that was all. Her uninvited guest had left empty-handed.

But this was something totally unexpected. When she hatched her plan for keeping the ingredients of the flies a secret, she'd never imagined anyone would go to such lengths trying to find the materials she used. The apparent success of her unlikely scheme was evidently going to entail a higher personal cost than she'd anticipated.

With that troubling thought, she went back inside, turned off the lights, and climbed back in bed.

Tuesday morning brought a new flood of orders, and she was still dealing with those when the telephone rang. She answered and recognized the voice of Jerry Vance, writer of the "Outdoor Oracle" column in the Fultonville *Advance*. "Hey, Vicki," he said, "I hear you've got a hot new fly. It's all over the Internet, and everybody's talking about it. I want to write about it in tomorrow's column. Can you help me out?"

"Happy to," Vicki said, thinking a little more publicity surely wouldn't hurt. "What do you want to know?"

He asked for names and descriptions of the patterns and she gave them. Then he said, "your website says you're selling only tied flies, not the pattern or the materials. What's with that?"

"Trade secrets. If I give out the pattern and sell the materials, then every fly tyer and his brother will be tying the flies, and I won't be able to sell any out of the shop. And I need to sell them to make a living."

"Gotcha. But some people won't like that."

"Believe me, I know. But that's the way it has to be."

They talked a little more, and Jerry promised the story would be in next day's paper, then asked if Vicki could email him a photo of the flies to use with the story. She agreed and sent him a copy of the photo posted on the shop website.

Well, that was good, she thought, then suddenly realized she wasn't alone. Jimmy the Geek was in the corner, again pretending to inspect the display of fly-tying materials. "Jimmy, I didn't hear you come in," she said. "Where've you been?"

"Busy," was all he said, approaching the counter. "But I thought you might need some help again."

Vicki paused for a moment. She didn't want to encourage him, but when she looked at the rising stack of orders ready to ship, she couldn't resist the temptation to ask if he would take them to the post office. Jimmy looked like a puppy that had just been given a treat. "Sure," he said. They made the usual arrangement and she helped him carry a couple of armloads of shipping envelopes to his Volkswagen.

Vicki looked at it doubtfully. "Does this thing still run?"

"Sure. How do you think I got here?"

She didn't answer, just handed him the money she'd taken from the till and told him to be careful. The car started with a series of explosions from the broken muffler and Jimmy headed for town.

Wednesday morning she could hardly wait to see the paper. It was delivered by mail to the shop and it would be two or three days before it arrived, but she knew it was also available online, so she booted up the computer, ignored the incoming emails and went straight to the *Advance* website and found the "Outdoor Oracle" column. The first thing she noticed was the photo she'd sent Jerry Vance was nowhere to be seen, which made her unhappy. Muttering a favorite obscenity, she began reading the column. The first two paragraphs were devoted to local fishing reports, but the third paragraph had what she was looking for: "Several of the anglers quoted above reported great success with some new fly patterns from Vicki Brightman at the Stub Mountain Fly Shop. Vicki inherited the shop recently from her father, the highly regarded Curly Brightman, who helped keep the fly boxes of local anglers stocked for many years. Now Vicki, a young lady who learned fly tying from her dad, is carrying on the tradition."

Wow, that was nice. He called her a young lady! She basked in the glow of that for a moment, then resumed reading:

"There are four patterns in Vicki's new series. They include three adult caddis imitations and a single imitation of a chironomid, whatever that is (we assume you fly guys know). There's lots of chatter on the Internet about how well these flies work, and it looks like Vicki has got herself some winners. She says they're selling fast and available only at the shop on Route 206. Don't bother asking for materials to tie your own, though; Vicki says 'they're a trade secret.'"

Well, that was pretty OK, Vicki thought. Maybe it will help sales. But she was still upset about the missing photo.

She saved the article on her computer and turned to the daily deluge of new orders. Sorting through them, she saw an email from the "Outdoor Oracle" and opened it. "Hey Vicki," it read, "I really appreciate your help yesterday and I hope you like the article. I'm really sorry the photo didn't appear with it; my nasty editor said it wouldn't fit on the page. Anyway, thanks again. Jerry."

Well, that made her feel a little better, and she settled down to begin processing orders.

The rest of the week was a blur. The *Advance* article brought an increase in orders, and Vicki was so busy she had to call Anne Walling in twice to watch the shop while she processed them, put the flies in shipping envelopes, printed address labels and stuck them on the envelopes, while also taking time out to dye another lot of goose feathers. Jimmy the Geek turned up two or three times, and she sent him twice to the post office in Fultonville. When he returned from the second trip he said, "I got you another present," and handed her a paper bag. The bag wasn't heavy, so it wasn't another jar of peanut butter. She opened it and found a loaf of bread. "Oh, Jimmy, you shouldn't have," she said, meaning it. The bread was sourdough, which she thought wouldn't go too well with peanut butter, but poor clueless Jimmy apparently didn't know that.

Jimmy's face turned crimson, but he couldn't think of anything to say.

Saturday was the busiest day yet, but when Jimmy turned up again, Vicki, against her better judgment, let him wait on a couple of customers while she continued wrestling with new orders. Each customer bought something and, as far as she could tell, Jimmy charged the right amounts and got the change correct.

Sunday brought more of the same and that night she resolved not to look at her computer or answer the phone while the shop was closed Monday. Instead, she got her waders, vest, and fly rod, jumped in her car, and drove up Route 206 to the Powder Horn National Forest. She parked near a favorite spot on Te-Hoosh Creek and spent several relaxing hours casting dry flies to rising trout. The flies, of course, were Stub Mountain caddis imitations, and she was gratified to find they actually *did* work, at least now and then. Most of the fish she caught were between ten and fourteen inches, about what she'd expected, but they were strong and vigorous and great fun on her seven-foot fly rod. She also enjoyed the sounds and fresh coolness of the stream, the scent of the forest, and the songs of many birds, including an especially noisy and persistent kingfisher. It didn't even bother her that it started raining before she left, feeling refreshed and ready to face whatever she found back at the shop.

Next morning she found the usual new orders on the Internet and her answering machine, but then came to a recorded phone message that surprised her. "This call is for Vicki Brightman," a male voice said. "This is Winston Bristow at *Tippets* magazine. We've been getting lots of emails and letters about your new series of flies and we'd like to interview you and do a story about the flies." He left a number and asked her to call back.

Well, how about that! She searched around, found the latest issue of *Tippets*, and looked at the masthead where she found Bristow listed as a "field editor." What the hell was that? How do you edit a field? She thumbed through the magazine and found an article with his byline. It was about a fly pattern she'd never heard of, but she read it anyway. It seemed well written and very detailed and was accompanied by close-up color photos showing each step of the tying process. At first she admired the photos, then felt a stab of alarm; if Winston Bristow, or whoever he was, wanted to do a story on her flies he'd want photos like these to put in the magazine. She couldn't allow that; it would reveal the materials she desperately wanted to keep secret.

But she couldn't just ignore the call, either, so she returned it. After introductions, Bristow told her he wanted to visit the Stub Mountain Fly Shop, interview her, get the story behind the flies, and photograph her tying one of them. Vicki agreed to everything except the photos, and the conversation went downhill from there. It ended with an annoyed Bristow telling her she was crazy if she thought she could keep the patterns and materials secret, even crazier if she turned down an offer of free publicity in a national fly-fishing magazine.

"That publicity could ruin my business," she said, and on that unhappy note they ended the call.

The conversation left her depressed. She replayed it several times in her mind, concluding each time that it couldn't have turned out any other way. With a heavy sigh, she decided she wouldn't think about it anymore, and returned to the daily chore of processing orders.

But the call continued bothering her until she realized it was only the latest of an expanding list of bothers. She was getting heartily tired of the tedium of processing orders, tired of dying goose feathers every week, tired of having people searching her garbage can or arguing about her secretive policies. She glanced around the shop and realized it didn't feel like the friendly place it had been when she and her dad worked together. Back then she'd enjoyed waiting on customers, talking and joking with them, helping them choose flies or other things they needed. That had been her social life, such as it was, and she missed it keenly.

The old saying "be careful what you wish for" came unbidden to her mind. Maybe it applied to her. She'd wanted desperately to get the shop back on a sound financial footing and her crazy, outlandish scheme seemed on the verge of doing that, but she was starting to think maybe the price was getting too high.

But there was more work to be done, so she tried to clear her mind and get back to it.

After another week of relentless work she forced herself to go to the shop on Monday morning and check for new orders instead of taking another day off. Maybe, if there aren't too many orders, I can still get in a few hours of fishing, she thought. She turned on the computer, went to her email and found eight new orders, which wasn't too bad; she could process those in an hour.

She was still scrolling through the emails when the phone rang, startling her. Who'd be calling Monday morning? Don't they know the shop is closed Mondays? She decided to let the call go to voicemail. She heard her own recorded greeting invite whoever was calling to leave a message. Then she heard an unfamiliar deep male voice. "Vicki, you probably don't remember me," it said, "but this is Jeff Keegan. I'm in the area and would like to talk to you about your new flies. We have lots of customers asking about them. I know you don't want to give away the patterns, but I thought we might be able to work out some sort of licensing agreement so we could sell them in our shops. Anyway, please give me a call."

She grabbed the phone and interrupted him as he was leaving a number. "Hello, Jeff. Of course I remember you. We met at the Fly Tackle Dealers Show in Denver years ago. It's great to hear from you."

"Well, I'm glad I caught you. Did you hear my message? I'm at the Seattle store for a few days, and I thought as long as I was in this part of the country I might come see you and talk about those new fly patterns of yours."

To hell with the fly patterns, Vicki thought; I'd just like to see *you*. But she knew she had to be cautious. "Well, I don't know about a licensing deal, but we can sure talk about it. And it would be wonderful to see you." *Jeez*, she thought, *should I have said "wonderful"*?

"Great. I could be there tomorrow or the next day, if either of those would work."

OMG, the place is an absolute mess. "You want to come here? I was thinking maybe we could meet in Fultonville and have lunch . . . or something."

"Well, if it isn't too much trouble, I'd love to see your shop. And the flies."

"OK, that'd be fine. Why don't you come here for lunch day after tomorrow? Say about 12:30 or 1. Would that work?"

"That's perfect. I'll look forward to seeing you then." And he rang off.

I'll look forward to seeing you, too, she thought.

But how the hell am I going to serve lunch? Curly's old office was too small and cluttered and the house was a mess; the sink was full of dirty dishes, the kitchen floor littered with goose feathers from all her dying jobs, and she hadn't dusted in weeks. There just hadn't been time, and there wouldn't be time enough before Wednesday; she had orders to fill and the shop to look after.

That reminded her the first thing she'd have to do was arrange for Anne Walling to watch the shop while she was hosting Keegan. That would solve one problem, but still left others.

Thoughts of fishing were forgotten and she started filling the new orders, following her procedure by rote while she wondered what to do. By the time she'd processed the eight new email orders plus a couple more from the phone, she'd come up with a plan.

She turned on the radio and listened for a weather forecast; Wednesday was supposed to be warm and clear. So far, so good. Then she went out to look at the picnic table next to the fly shop. Curly had installed it on the side away from the highway so drop-in customers could have lunch if they wished, although few ever had. Now it was covered with pine needles and bird droppings.

Returning to the shop, Vicki approached her next task with trepidation because it meant she had to call Jimmy the Geek. But she did anyway and asked if he'd be available to run to the post office in Fultonville the next day, then pick up a big order for her from Groppo's Delicatessen.

"Awesome," he said.

After that she went back to the house, found a good plastic tablecloth and a collection of wooden discs cut from a lodgepole pine that she could use to hold down the corners and put them near the front door. Then she filled a bucket with hot water and took it, an old washcloth, a can of Comet, and a broom and returned to the picnic table. She swept off the thick layer of pine needles and scrubbed away the bird droppings until the tabletop fairly gleamed. When that was done she returned to the house, found an old sheet and covered the table so it wouldn't be covered with a fresh layer of needles and bird droppings by Wednesday afternoon.

One more thing—no, make it two. Back in the house she unearthed two old coolers, cleaned them, and put them near the front door. Then she sat down at the hopelessly cluttered dining-room table and made a menu: Seasoned fried chicken, potato salad, beer, pop, bottled water, pickles, and several other items. She looked up the number for Groppo's Delicatessen and put it at the top of the list.

There. That should do it. Oh, except for utensils and napkins. She hurriedly washed some utensils and put them in the dish drainer, then searched for some paper napkins. Finding none, she added them to the list for Jimmy to take to the delicatessen.

Whew. She looked at her watch and was surprised to find it was already noon. I could have been fishing instead of doing all this, she thought.

But maybe it would be worth it. She remembered what a handsome hunk Jeff Keegan had been when she first met him. And wealthy besides! She could hardly wait to see him.

She made herself a peanut butter sandwich for lunch and was disconcerted to find a dyed green goose feather in the middle of it. She really did have to sweep the kitchen floor.

Wednesday morning she spent more than the ordinary time in front of the bathroom mirror, working on her face and hair. When she surveyed the results she was forced to conclude that she looked like a forty-two-year-old woman, not the young, pretty girl she had been when she first met Jeff Keegan. She wondered if he still remembered her the way she was then; if so, he was bound to be disappointed when he saw her now.

For that matter, maybe she'd be disappointed, too. She realized her mind still held an image of him as he was when they first met, many years ago. What if he'd changed? Was she foolish to be so anxious and excited to see him? Should she prepare herself for disappointment, just in case?

No, she decided. That was too negative a thought—especially on such a gorgeous summer morning. The forecast had been exactly right.

It took forever for the morning to pass. She tackled the usual overnight backlog of orders, welcomed Anne Walling to the shop, brought her up to speed, then busied herself making final preparations for Keegan's visit. She returned to the house to put ice in the two coolers, then took the fried chicken, potato salad, and drinks from the refrigerator and placed them on top of the ice. She added plastic plates, utensils, and napkins, then carried the coolers to the picnic table and left them in the shade on one of the table's benches. There was still nearly an hour left before noon when she finished, so she went back inside the shop and started doing what she always did when she was nervous: She sat down at Curly's old vise and started tying flies. Anne watched her curiously, wondering why she'd been summoned when it appeared Vicki had time on her hands. For her part, Vicki was hardly conscious of what she was doing; if someone had asked her what pattern she was tying, she wouldn't have been able to answer.

It seemed forever before her watch told her it was 12:30. She put away the fly-tying stuff and walked to the front of the shop, where she could see the highway through the window and waited, watching and feeling ever more nervous. She'd told Jeff to come between 12:30 and 1, and as the minutes passed slowly she began feeling resentful he hadn't yet appeared. If he was really anxious to see her, he should have arrived at 12:30 on the dot, maybe even earlier. Was the fact that he hadn't a sign that he *wasn't* anxious to see her? She couldn't help thinking so, and as the minute hand on her watch dragged slowly toward 1 o'clock, the thought grew even stronger.

It was six minutes past the hour, and she was wondering if maybe she'd been stood up when a gray Toyota pulled into one of the parking spaces in front of the shop. She saw the sticker on its windshield identifying it as a rental. The driver's-side door opened and Jeff Keegan stepped out.

At least it looked vaguely like Jeff Keegan, though not the one she remembered. The first thing she noticed was he'd gained weight; that was evident not only around his midsection but also on his once-handsome face, which was now puffy, especially around the eyes.

The second thing she noticed was that he was wearing a wedding ring.

All her pent-up excitement and anxiety suddenly collapsed like a punctured balloon, and she realized her fantasies had been exactly that—fantasies.

Keegan wore gray slacks and a blue fishing shirt with his company logo embroidered over the left-hand pocket. He saw Vicki waiting at the shop door and advanced with a big grin on his face. She opened the door, smiled as best she could in return, and thought about giving him a big hug, but something held her back.

Maybe it was the wedding ring.

They settled for a handshake and a few words of small talk about his trip, the weather, and so on, and she took him on a brief tour of the shop. He nodded several times in apparent approval but said nothing, and when she had shown him everything she suggested it was time for lunch and led him outside to the picnic table.

Groppo's had come through again. The cold fried chicken and potato salad were excellent, and they each had a beer with the meal. Jeff offered belated condolences over Curly's passing and they compared notes on other mutual acquaintances until the plates covered with chicken bones were shoved aside and they got down to business.

"I told you on the phone that we keep getting inquiries about your flies, and my shop managers say we've got to get some," Jeff said, "so as I told you, I'm hoping we could come to some sort of licensing agreement so we can sell the flies in our shops."

"How would that work?"

"Well, what I had in mind is that you would give us a license to advertise and sell the Stub Mountain flies and we'd keep a small percentage of the sale price—that could be negotiated. Your tyers would provide the flies, and that way you could keep the patterns and the materials confidential. I think it could be a good deal for both of us."

Vicki frowned. "Three problems," she said. "First, there's no way my tyers could provide that many flies; we can hardly keep up with the business we have here, which I'm sure is a lot less than yours. Second, I'd have to charge you close to full price for each fly in order to pay my tiers and purchase the materials they use. And finally, if your three big shops started selling my flies, it would probably ruin my business; those flies account for a lot of it."

"Well, I don't see any of those as insoluble," he said. "I have lots of contract tyers at my disposal and the licensing agreement could be written to include permission for them to tie the flies as long as they kept the patterns secret. That way I'd absorb the cost of paying the tiers and buying the materials, and with the sales volume we have, I think you'd end up making more money than you do now."

That's what he's really after, Vicki thought; he just wants the patterns. She shook her head.

They sparred for another quarter hour, with Keegan making more suggestions and Vicki rejecting each until it was obvious they had reached an impasse. "Well," he said, draining the last of his second beer, "I'm sorry it turned out this way; I was really hoping we could come to some sort of agreement." He paused and looked around at the shop and the home behind it. "How much property do you have here, Vicki?"

"A little over six acres. Why?"

"Well, I was just thinking. Would you be interested in selling?"

The idea hit her like a lightning bolt. "You can't be serious."

"Why not? I've been looking for another property, and I like what I see here."

"But you have three big shops in three big cities. Why on earth would you want this little place out in the sticks?"

"Actually, I think this is a pretty good location, right on the high-way leading to all the fishing in the Powder Horn Forest. I'm sure you get a lot of drop-in traffic and I'd expect that to continue. And if you have that much property, I might just put in a burger joint next to the fly shop. Then we'd get that much more drop-in traffic. The two would feed off each other."

Vicki thought Jeff looked like he'd already had enough hamburg-ers, but she kept it to herself. "Well, if you're really serious about this, I'll have to think about it," she said.

"I am serious, and of course I'd expect you to think about it. But the flies would have to be part of the deal—both the dressings and the materials."

"Yeah, I get that."

"So why don't we do this: While you're thinking about your options, and if it's OK with you, I'd like to send an appraiser out here to have a good look at the place—the property, the physical plant, utilities, all that good stuff. He's done work for me before and he's really good at it. He'll have to spend some time poking around, but he's pretty low-key and I don't think he'll get in your way. Then, depending on what he has to tell me and what you've decided, we can get together again and work out the details. Or, if not, nothing ventured."

Vicki thought for a moment. "OK," she said finally. "I guess that would be all right."

They shook hands, Jeff thanked her for the lunch, told her it was great to see her again—she secretly thought he might have been as disappointed as she was—and drove away in his rented Toyota.

She watched him go and asked herself what she'd just done. Still seated at the picnic table, she opened another beer and tried to think. Did she really want to sell the place? Her shop, her home for all forty-two years of her life, the business she had worked so hard to bring to back to life? The very notion brought a feeling of cold panic.

But on the other hand, did she want to spend the rest of her working life processing orders for flies? Arguing with people over the
patterns? Chasing them out of her garbage can? Fending off Jimmy
the Geek? Living out her days in the boondocks? She realized she'd
hardly ever been anywhere—the long-ago trip to the Fly Tackle Dealers Show in Denver was the only one she could remember. Was it
time to move on, see something of the world, have some adventures?
Fish new waters and catch new fish?

She didn't find the answer in the beer bottle, though the beer tasted
good.

If anyone had later asked Vicki what she did during the remainder
of the week, she wouldn't have been able to remember. Preoccupied
with thoughts about her future, she went about her work mechanically,
then lay awake at night, still thinking. The decision came slowly, a
little at a time, and even then she had to wait for it to settle until it felt
comfortable. By Monday, with the shop closed, she decided she was
ready and made the call to Jeff Keegan. She tried hard not to sound
nervous when she told him she was ready to sell.

"That's great!" he said. "I was hoping that would be your decision." He told her he'd be sending a man named Albert Rodosovich,
his appraiser, to look at the place. "He should be there before the end
of the week."

Rodosovich arrived Thursday. He was a small man with slumping
shoulders and a slumping face, a scrim of fuzzy hair bordering the
edges of a mostly bald pate, and rheumy eyes behind a pair of wire-
rimmed glasses. He went about his work quietly and unobtrusively, as
Keegan had promised, but with an intensity that was almost frightening. He checked everything—the well, pumphouse and water system,
the pipes, the septic system, the gutters and downspouts, the Internet
speed, the electrical system, the chimneys, roofs and foundations of
the shop and home, the property deed, the annual assessments and

taxes, and measured everything down to the last millimeter. Vicki had the shop inventory on her computer and he copied that onto a flash drive. He even visited the county courthouse in Fultonville to inquire about procedures for obtaining building permits. During all that time he scarcely said a word to Vicki, and he left without giving her a clue as to his findings.

But she found out the following week when Keegan called and said he was ready to make an offer. "I think we should get together and talk about this," he said, "and if we can come to an agreement, then we should bring in the lawyers and let them handle it."

"Sounds good to me," she said.

They set a date for the meeting, and Vicki called Jimmy and Anne Walling to watch the shop while she cleaned house from top to bottom, especially the dining room where she planned to hold the meeting over another lunch imported from Groppo's. This time, however, there were no fantasies; it would all be strictly business.

She gulped when Keegan made his offer. It was more than she'd expected, more than she'd thought the place was worth, surely enough for her to start a new life without having to worry about her bank account.

But he wasn't finished. "I want to make it clear, though, that the offer includes the property, the shop, the house, *and* disclosure of the Stub Mountain patterns and materials, plus the right to make and sell the flies. That's one of the main reasons the offer is as high as it is; otherwise, we won't have a deal."

"Understood," Vicki said. "That's not a problem. But there's one little thing."

"What's that?"

"The kid who's watching the shop now, Jimmy the Geek. He's kind of a pest, but he's also very useful; he set up our website, he's learned to wait on customers and he's very handy making runs to Fultonville. I have no idea if he will want to stay here after I leave, but if so, I'd appreciate it if you could try to find a place for him."

"I'll think about it," Keegan said.

They shook hands, agreed to call in the lawyers to take care of the paperwork, then meet one last time to sign the papers and turn over the secrets of the Stub Mountain flies.

The meeting took place two weeks later between just the two of them. They signed the papers where the attorneys had indicated and Keegan produced a check for the agreed amount. "This is yours after you give me the information about the flies," he said.

"Sure," Vicki said, handing him two sheets of paper on which she'd printed the dressings of the four patterns. The name of Major Neely was never mentioned; Vicki didn't want anyone looking in the old book she'd found in her dad's library.

Keegan studied the patterns. "Dyed goose flank feathers," he said finally. "Well, I'll be damned. When you trim them all the way down like that, they almost look and feel like fur of some kind. No wonder nobody could figure it out." He looked at her in admiration. "But what makes the flies so effective?"

"They aren't," Vicki said. "They're no more effective than any other fly."

"Huh? What about all those fabulous reports on the Internet and stuff?"

"Well, let's just say I helped that along a little bit."

"What do you mean?"

"Some of those Internet reports and tweets weren't exactly true."

"Huh? You mean they were phony?"

"Phony is a harsh word. Let me put it this way: Did you ever hear a fishing report that *was* entirely true? That wasn't exaggerated? Maybe those Internet reports were just exaggerated a little more than usual."

"And that was *you*?"

Vicki just smiled.

"Well, I'll be damned." A slow, sly smile formed on his face. "Vicki, you're a real piece of work."

She said nothing.

"And you say these flies really aren't any better than any others?"

"That's right."

"Then what about all the great online fishing reports you *didn't* write? There must have been some. How do you explain those?"

"Easy. If you have confidence in a fly, you keep using it, and sooner or later a fish will take any fly you use. That's what happened with the Stub Mountain flies; people kept using them until they finally started catching fish, and they figured the fly pattern had to be the reason why."

Keegan shook his head. "You know, Vicki, if you don't mind my saying so, this—what you did, those phony reports and all—wasn't that a bit unethical?"

"Not at all. Just think about it: The whole premise of fly fishing is to offer a phony imitation to a trout so it will rise and take it. What could be more appropriate, or more ethical, than to do the same thing to trout fishermen? That's all I did."

Keegan absorbed that and frowned. "You know," he said, "this could screw up our whole deal."

"I don't think so," Vicki replied. "You already signed the papers."

Vicki awoke to a soft, warm breeze coming through the louvered windows and lay awake listening to the sound of surf breaking on the distant reef. She could tell from the streaks of light coming through the louvers that the sun was already well above the horizon and it would be another warm day. She stretched, got out of bed, plugged in the coffeemaker, and took the first steaming cup out on the screened-in porch of her rented Bahamian bungalow. She sat in a comfortable chair, took her first sip of coffee and watched the tide flooding slowly across the coral flat in front of the bungalow.

She felt her spirits rising along with the tide. It would soon be high enough to start fishing, and she would wade to the spot where yesterday she'd hooked six bonefish and landed four. The smallest, a little more than fourteen inches long, astonished her when it ripped off at least forty yards of backing on its first run. How could such a small fish do that? But the others ran even farther. She'd always loved the trout she caught in the waters of the Powder Horn National Forest, but these bonefish were something else. They had an extra gear. No, make that two extra gears.

Remembering those Powder Horn trout made her wonder for a moment how things were going back at the Stub Mountain Fly Shop. Had Keegan started construction on his burger joint? Were the Stub Mountain flies still selling briskly? Was Jimmy still geeking?

But those thoughts lasted only a moment before she dismissed them and made an abrupt decision: It was time to add the Stub Mountain Fly Shop to the list of things she'd never think about again. Right up there at the top of the list next to Roger.

THE FISHLEXIC

IT CAME as no surprise to anyone when Dr. Timothy Hardhorn received the Nobel Prize. Nearly everybody agreed he deserved it for his revolutionary discovery of the genetic origins of early-onset dementia, thus opening new paths of therapy that promised to brighten and expand the lives of countless people.

It also helped that Dr. Hardhorn was exceedingly photogenic, with a ruggedly handsome face, clear blue eyes, a killer smile, and scientifically fashionable long hair. He had an interesting résumé, too; he'd helped pay for his college education working as custodian of a flock of penguins incarcerated at the local zoo, established a reputation as a relentlessly aggressive poker player, and was well known as an ardent fly fisherman, a pastime widely considered socially acceptable. It was as easy to find a photograph of him dressed in waders at streamside as it was to find one of him wearing a lab coat and peering into a binocular microscope.

Not long after receiving the Nobel Prize he also married Heidi Drummond, a lovely, high-profile supermodel whose ample accoutrements had several times been on full-color display in *Sports Illustrated*'s annual swimsuit issue. The Hardhorn-Drummond union received the unanimous approval of the supermarket tabloids, which soon started referring to the newlyweds as "Tim and Heidi," as if they were everybody's intimate friends. The editors also were especially fond of the "penguin angle," although Dr. Hardhorn had carefully refrained from telling them he secretly relieved several penguins of some of their waterproof wing feathers, which he used to tie his personal favorite dry-fly pattern, the Emperor.

As a result of all the publicity, "Tim and Heidi" found themselves pursued by paparazzi nearly everywhere they went, which was annoying. Except for that, however, it seemed there was nothing more in life Dr. Hardhorn could possibly desire.

Yet there was one thing. The good doctor was acutely aware that three of his closest fishing friends had suffered extreme disappointment when their sons grew up without displaying even the slightest interest in fly fishing, or fishing of any sort. All three men had been looking forward keenly to the companionship of a fly-fishing son, and Dr. Hardhorn was determined to avoid the same disappointment. That's why he'd spent several years collecting DNA samples from prominent fly fishers under the guise of helping them trace their ancestry. Donors included such luminaries as Oliver Dobbs, the British fly fisher and author of the popular book *Chalk Stream Dreams*, and Buck Norris, the homely but amiable host of a long-running television series about saltwater fly fishing. Hardhorn had even managed to obtain a DNA sample from Clint Steele, the world's most famous fly fisher, whose ancestry he traced to a notorious family of Maltese pirates.

So, after a year of marriage, when Heidi told her husband she was pregnant, he was well prepared.

The tabloids got excited all over again with the news of her pregnancy, but as usual they didn't have the full story, which was that with his wife's assent Dr. Hardhorn had secretly "edited" the DNA in their child's embryo to make sure neither it nor any of its progeny ever would fall victim to early-onset dementia. But Heidi didn't get the full story, either; Dr. Hardhorn never told her he'd made a few other genetic adjustments to the embryo. With the samples he'd obtained from famous anglers, it was fairly easy for him to isolate the genes necessary to produce a male child who would grow up with an irresistible impulse to become a fanatical fly fisher, so he secretly juggled the genes in Heidi's embryo to assure just such an outcome.

Why not? He couldn't see any harm in it, and it would assure he'd always have a fly-fishing son to keep him company on the stream. He knew it was best to keep the matter under wraps, however, for there were still those in the scientific and medical communities and the public at large who thought tampering with the genetic makeup of human embryos was unethical, or worse.

Nine months later, when little Rodney Hardhorn made his entry into the world, he was a perfectly normal child from all outward appearances, and by the time he was three years old it was obvious he was very precocious. At that age, after watching his father tie a Gray Hackle Peacock, he tied one himself. To be sure, it was a simple pattern and it looked a trifle lopsided, but hey, the kid was only three years old, and nobody had ever heard of another child tying a fly at such a tender age. Dr. Hardhorn was so proud and impressed he didn't even notice that Rodney had tied the fly on a hook one size smaller than the one his father used.

Two years later, after making a perfect cast, Rodney hooked and landed his first trout on a fly he tied himself. By age seven he had mastered the double haul, and a year after that he started writing fly-fishing stories. By the time he was a teenager he'd won several casting competitions, established his own fly-tying business specializing in very small flies, and, most important, was fishing alongside his father at every possible opportunity. To Dr. Hardhorn's great pride and satisfaction, his hope for a son who would be his lifelong fishing companion seemed fulfilled.

It was only when Rodney reached his late teens that Dr. Hardhorn first noticed something a little unusual about his son. The two had spent a pleasant day fishing a small stream not known for producing large trout, but on the trip home Rodney kept talking excitedly about the sixteen-inch rainbow he'd caught on a size 18 dry fly—a giant fish for that stream and a noteworthy catch under any circumstances. Dr. Hardhorn had witnessed the catch, though, and was certain the trout wasn't more than fourteen inches long, if even that. He also remembered the fly was a size 14.

But he said nothing.

On their next trip, to a different river, Rodney landed a handsome brown trout that Dr. Hardhorn estimated weighed about 2½ pounds, though Rodney insisted it was at least a pound heavier. They had spent part of the day fishing out of sight of one another, but Rodney's claim that he'd landed a total of nineteen trout also seemed unlikely to his father, who'd struggled to capture less than half that number.

Again, however, he said nothing. After all, it didn't seem a big deal; wasn't every fisherman prone to exaggerate the size and number of his catch from time to time? Or maybe even all the time? Dr. Hardhorn occasionally had been guilty of that himself, though he always felt remorseful afterward; as a scientist, he felt obliged to tell the truth about things he observed in his work. But fly fishing was play, not work, so what was the harm in a little exaggeration? Besides, Rodney had become such a skilled fisherman by then it was hardly surprising if he sometimes caught more or bigger fish than his father, even if the evidence sometimes seemed to indicate the contrary. A habit of occasionally exaggerating fish size or numbers seemed a minor character flaw, one Dr. Hardhorn thought could be easily overlooked. What if his son had turned out to be a ballet dancer, or a Republican, or something equally vile, instead of a fly fisherman? The doctor decided he should forget the exaggerations and just count his blessings.

Besides, he had other concerns. Heidi had suffered a monumental bout of postpartum depression after Rodney's birth and was acting as if it had never completely worn off, becoming increasingly grumpy and withdrawn. Dr. Hardhorn suggested counseling, but she dismissed the idea immediately, so he decided to consult a counselor himself and see if he could learn what was bothering her. Based on his description of her symptoms and behavior, the counselor suggested she was feeling depressed because she was no longer the center of attention she had been as a supermodel. Her spectacular figure had never quite recovered from her pregnancy, so her image was no longer in demand. The paparazzi that had once annoyed her no longer followed her around and now she missed them, the tabloids had forgotten their dear friends "Tim and Heidi," and the rest of the fickle world seemed to have moved on.

The counselor's diagnosis was that Heidi felt neglected. His not-so-subtle suggestion was that Dr. Hardhorn should consider spending more time with his wife and perhaps less time fishing with his son.

Trying to take that suggestion to heart, the doctor made what he thought was a good-faith effort to give his wife more attention, but it didn't last long. After all, it was the middle of trout season, and . . . well, his son wanted to go fishing. Actually, his son's father did, too.

So that's what they did. It wasn't very long, however, before the doctor's other fishing companions began to notice and express annoyance at the glaring inflations in Rodney's fishing reports. Ed Nichols, Dr. Hardhorn's oldest fishing friend—one of those who was so disappointed his own son didn't become a fly fisherman—telephoned after a trip the three had made together and came right to the point.

"You've got to have a talk with Rodney," he said. "I hate to tell you this, but that kid can't tell a ten-inch trout from a can of beans. He exaggerates the size of every fish he catches, and fibs about how many fish he catches, too. He always says he caught more than anybody else and they were all bigger, and he always says he caught them on a fly two or three sizes smaller than the one he really used. I know because I've seen him do it—and so have you. I mean, a little exaggeration once in a while is OK; we all do it, even me. But your son is ridiculous. He's going to get a bad reputation. I mean it; you have to talk to him, try to reel him in a little."

Dr. Hardhorn was a little startled at the aggressiveness of his friend's tirade but had to admit he was on target. "You're right," he said when he could finally get a word in edgewise. "I've seen the same thing myself, and I guess it is getting a little out of hand. I'll talk to him, see if I can get him straightened out."

Which he did, but the conversation did not go well for either of them. Somewhat to his father's surprise, Rodney fervently denied ever inflating the number or size of the fish he caught, or reducing the size of the flies he used to catch them, and they each ended up raising their voices and angrily saying a few things they might later regret. Tension lingered in the air for days afterward, during which they hardly spoke to one another.

It didn't help that things still weren't exactly rosy for Dr. Hardhorn elsewhere on the domestic front. Heidi had lately become even more surly and withdrawn, and Dr. Hardhorn still wasn't sure he understood why; he thought he'd made a reasonable effort to pacify her. But his once happy household was now beginning to resemble the 38th Parallel in Korea, and the only way he could think of relieving his own anxiety over the situation was, as always, to go fishing, hoping a relaxing day on the water might help him forget his domestic problems.

Somewhat to his surprise, however, Rodney wasn't enthusiastic about going with him. Usually all the doctor had to say was "Let's go fishing" and Rodney would run to get his gear. Not this time. It took several minutes of argument and Hardhorn's reluctant concession that he wouldn't again bring up the issue of Rodney's exaggerations before his son finally agreed to go.

It turned out to be anything but a relaxing day on the stream. The trout tried willingly to do their part, but there was still a lot of tension between father and son, and it hadn't subsided by the time they got home. Dr. Hardhorn felt just as unhappy as he'd been earlier.

After that things went downhill rapidly. Heidi's unexplained behavior increased steadily until there was virtually no communication remaining between them, and then came the morning when she abruptly announced she was leaving, which she promptly did, despite his anguished pleas for explanation. A week later she sued him for divorce on grounds of "abandonment," specifically citing loss of companionship because her husband was always either away at work or out fishing. When he called her to propose reconciliation or at least a joint appointment with a marriage counselor, she curtly told him any future communication would have to be through her attorney.

That, as it turned out, would be the last time he would ever talk to her. And at a time when he needed his son's support and companionship more than ever, Rodney remained almost as aloof and distant as his mother had been. When the divorce was granted, the judge added even more to Dr. Hardhorn's anguish by ordering him to pay staggering sums of alimony.

With his life apparently crumbling on every front, Dr. Hardhorn considered his options and eventually decided the only course remaining was to try to reconcile with his son. He set the stage for what he hoped would be a peaceful discussion by building a fire in the fireplace and pouring a full snifter of brandy for each of them, but that merely seemed to put Rodney on guard. The doctor's carefully rehearsed and reasoned plea—that his son needed to rein in his fishing exaggerations or risk loss of his reputation—also got no response. Rodney might have been stone deaf, or maybe even made of stone.

As a last resort, Dr. Hardhorn went into the kitchen, got a steelhead out of the freezer and placed it next to a yardstick and scale in front of Rodney. His son had taken the steelhead a week earlier and said it measured forty-one inches and weighed twenty-one pounds when caught. He also claimed he'd taken it on a size 22 dry fly, which seemed highly doubtful to his father. When measured against the yardstick, the fish was actually only thirty-one inches from nose to tail, and according to the scale it weighed nine pounds, four ounces. Of course it had been cleaned and out of the water for a week so it was bound to weigh less than when it was caught, but there was no possible way it ever could have measured forty-one inches or weighed even close to twenty-one pounds. Dr. Hardhorn also happened to know it had been caught on a size 6 Green-butt Skunk, a steelhead fly.

Yet even when confronted with this incontrovertible evidence, Rodney hotly refused to accept it. He studied the fish, the scale, and the yardstick and Dr. Hardhorn watched his lips move as he silently parsed the numbers and tried to assimilate them. He could see his son was trying to make a good-faith effort but was struggling to understand the numbers in front of him. Finally, Rodney said, "I don't know what the hell you're talking about! That fish clearly measures forty-one inches, and the scale says it weighs twenty-one pounds. And if you want me to show you the size 22 fly it took, I'll go and get it. Now, for crying out loud, get off my back!"

That was the moment Dr. Hardhorn realized Rodney had a real problem: he was congenitally incapable of recognizing or understanding the numbers on the yardstick or the scale. He obviously had an extraordinary form of dyslexia, a tiny, short circuit or some other aberration in the cerebral wiring that causes distortion in one's ability to perceive or understand words, symbols or sounds, sometimes even making people "see" things backward.

What's more, Dr. Hardhorn knew why; his own genetic tinkering was responsible. The DNA that made his son grow up to become a fly fisher also apparently contained something else that made it impossible for him to interpret fish sizes, weights or numbers correctly; he really did believe his steelhead measured forty-one inches and weighed twenty-one pounds; in his mind's eye there was no doubt.

But the confrontation had left both men frustrated and red-hot angry and there was no way Rodney was in a mood to hear such an explanation—not that Dr. Hardhorn was anxious to give him one anyway—so they parted company without another word.

Next day the doctor found himself alone; Rodney had packed his fishing gear and other possessions and departed overnight, leaving no word where he was going.

Left by himself in a state of deepening depression, Dr. Hard-horn could think of nothing else except to fall back on his scientific training. He tried to analyze what had gone wrong with the genetic enhancement of Rodney so he could chronicle it for posterity, eventually preparing a long, detailed monograph in which he defined a new ailment he called "Fishlexia," whose symptoms seemed to apply only to male fly fishers and included the inability to recognize the true length or weight of a fish, the number of fish one caught, or the size of the fly used to catch them. Several respected medical journals rejected the article, but it finally appeared in an obscure publication called the *Mississippi Journal of Medicine & Catfish Farming*, which was not widely read by people in the scientific or medical communities.

Maybe that was just as well. Over the years Dr. Hardhorn's reputation as a Nobel laureate had lost much of its luster when he failed to deliver any further sensational discoveries. His personal trials also had left him no longer as good looking or photogenic as he once was; his scientifically fashionably long hair had whitened, his blue eyes were bloodshot and undercut by dark purple crescents, and his killer smile now curved in the opposite direction. In hopeless despair, he finally disposed of his fly-fishing tackle in a garage sale, moved out of the house he no longer needed, and quietly dropped out of sight.

For his part, Rodney Hardhorn continued fly fishing in the manner of a hopeless addict, never realizing his genes gave him no choice in the matter. He fished hard almost every day from dawn till dusk, a lonely figure who had grown into the habit of talking to himself because he had no fishing companions. Once in a while, however, he'd bump into one of his father's old fishing friends, who would ask whatever became of his once-famous father.

Rodney's answer was always the same: "Last I heard he was in a retirement home somewhere in California. They were treating him for early-onset dementia."

DIARY OF AN UNKNOWN ANGLER

MY NAME is Andrew Royster. My academic colleagues and friends—
the few I have—call me Andy, or sometimes the "Modern Monk."
That's because I've dedicated myself to a career of study, reflection,
research, and writing. I am most comfortable in libraries, old book-
stores, and other quiet places, such as small ponds and little rivers
inhabited by trout. For, you see, my field of scholarship and academic
endeavor is the stuff of angling, primarily fly fishing, and all that has
been learned and written and said about it since the beginning of
recorded time.

I spend most of my life in a cluttered little office on the campus
of a private institution known as Marston University. My class on
angling history and literature is one of few taught in any college or
university in North America, perhaps in the world, for where else but
in a private college with many wealthy fly-fishing alumni could you
possibly have such a class?

I also devote part of my time to a small business, a little shop
called "Hooked on Books" that specializes in—what else?—classic
fishing books. The shop was originally opened by my uncle, but after
his untimely death my aunt handed it off to me. At first I thought of it

merely as an added burden, but after a while I became infatuated with the search for old, out-of-print fishing titles; it was rather like fishing itself, because when I finally found one I was looking for it gave me a sense of excitement parallel to catching a trout. I know that may sound like hyperbole, but it's the truth.

Sometimes I found myself sitting for long periods in the shop, listening to its old wooden walls creak and groan and imagining I could also hear the distant voices of many of the authors whose works rest on the shop's shelves—Dame Juliana delicately whispering that fly fishing is for one's physical and spiritual health, not for the increasing of their money, or old Izaak reminding everyone that God never made anything better than strawberries or angling, or the voices of Halford and Skues raised in righteous debate over which was better, the upstream dry fly or the nymph. Sometimes I even thought I could hear the lyrical, poetic voice of Roderick Haig-Brown, whose rivers never slept.

The business always had been marginal, but having reached an unexpected degree of satisfaction as its owner, I decided to try to keep it going. However, since I couldn't spend too much time away from my academic responsibilities, I was forced to hire two part-time employees to look after the place during the five days a week it was open. Their most important qualifications were their love of books and their willingness to work for very modest wages.

If there's such a thing as a stereotypical librarian, my two employees both fit the description. The older one, Ann Sebastian, once actually was a librarian at a small rural library in Southern Illinois. That's just about all I know about her, except that she lives in an apartment with two cats and seems to have no interest other than books. She's also several years older than I am, and that, plus the fact that she's a woman, seems to have given her license to treat me with a consistent attitude of faint contempt, even though I am her employer. Sometimes the attitude is not so faint. But I'm more than willing to put up with it because Sebastian's encyclopedic memory has made her indispensable; she apparently has memorized the location of every book on the store's meager shelves. My uncle left them badly disorganized, so Sebastian's knowledge has become vital to the business.

During her years of employment she also has cultivated an expert knowledge of fly fishing and its history, which also is invaluable. A tall, thin woman with streaks of gray in her long dark hair, she displays a perpetually menacing expression softened only a little by the granny glasses she wears. She looks like the type of librarian who would smack you on the knuckles with a wooden ruler if you raised your voice in her library. As you may have noticed, I always call her Sebastian, never Ann, and she seems to prefer it that way; it helps define our relationship, in which she always regards herself the superior.

My other employee is Vivian Foster, who also looks like a librarian but never actually was one. She's much younger than Sebastian, somewhere in her late twenties, and she was still in college when I hired her. She stayed on after graduation when she discovered her degree in English literature had little value in the job market. She's also tall and thin with uncontrollable dark curly hair and a soft round face with a turned-up nose, and she wears huge glasses that make her look something like an owl. She also lives alone in an apartment and is a strict vegetarian who reads many books about fruits, vegetables, and obscure Eastern religions. She's good with customers and handles much of the walk-in trade, although I've had to rebuff her frequent suggestions that we should begin stocking books about fruits, vegetables and obscure Eastern religions along with our fly-fishing books.

That's just about all I know about her. I suppose my idea of good employee relations, if I have one, is to ask them nothing and volunteer nothing beyond the minimum necessary for operation of the shop, so even after years of daily contact we remain almost strangers to one another. Sebastian usually works Mondays through Wednesdays and Vivian takes Thursdays and Fridays, although she's also available to fill in if Sebastian needs to take time off. I stop by at irregular intervals, whenever my schedule allows.

The shop itself is old. Or did I say that? It was built back in the days when there was lots of good wood still to be had, and it has held up well through the years until now it has a rich, dark patina that lends an air of dignity to the place. Sebastian brought a high-powered vacuum cleaner into the shop one day and sucked up enormous amounts of hair from the thin crevices in the hardwood floor, which leads me to suspect the place might once have been a barbershop—three chairs, no waiting. It has a single large plate-glass window, now partly filled with a small display of old books (nothing rare), and a heavy glass door. Most of the shop is occupied by bookshelves, one of them a series of glassed-in locking cases for the most valuable books. On one side of the store is a narrow counter where we have a cash register, phone, and computer terminal. In the rear is a tiny restroom and an equally tiny office with another computer that hosts our website, where most of our business is done.

Two of the inside walls are mostly bare except for a few scattered prints of old angling scenes, but the wall behind the counter features an enlargement of a famous black-and-white photograph from a century before, an image of Theodore Gordon, who many considered the patron saint of fly fishing in America, wading a stream with his female companion, whose name has been lost to history. In the photo the young woman appears as tall as the diminutive Gordon, perhaps taller, and she was dressed in a long garment; I don't know enough about women's fashions to call it a dress or a sheath or what, although I don't think it could be called a gown. Whatever it was, it nearly touched the water as she waded downstream. She also wore a large round hat that disclosed only a trace of what might have been dark hair. She was holding a long, limber fly rod that was bent sharply, and at the far edge of the photo was the blurred image of what appeared to be a struggling trout on the end of her line.

Gordon marched behind her, as near as her shadow, holding a fly rod at right-shoulder arms and carrying a creel over his left shoulder. He was nattily dressed as if he were going to church, although perhaps the river was his church. He seemed almost to hover next to her, perhaps ready to reach out and hold her upright if she should slip on a slick stone. It was a tranquil fishing scene that I thought a perfect centerpiece for my little shop.

It was unusual for all three of us to be in the shop at the same time, but on this particular morning we were all there, down on our knees behind the counter, frantically sifting through a pile of old books. If someone had walked into the store just then he or she might have thought an armed robbery was in progress and we had all been ordered down on the floor. But it wasn't a holdup that had us there; we were digging through a dozen battered cardboard boxes filled with books that smelled as old as they looked.

I'd purchased the books a day earlier from the owner of an antique store who decided to retire because she was becoming something of an antique herself. There were several hundred books in all, but I was really interested in only two—an extremely rare copy of Angus McCain's 1856 work, *Creating Flies for Trout*, and Jonathan Forge's scarce 1922 edition of *With Fly Rod in India*. The antique shop owner had insisted on selling the books only as an entire lot and I had finally agreed on a price of $500 for the whole collection. I knew it was a steal because the antique lady had no idea what she had; the Forge book wasn't very good, but it was rare and probably worth at least $500, and the McCain might fetch as much as twenty times more from a collector. That was the kind of thing that got me excited, like a big trout rising to my fly, and I wasn't troubled by any ethical considerations; I knew from experience that any rare book dealer would do the same.

As soon as I'd unloaded the books from the back of my van in the alley behind the store I removed the McCain and Forge volumes, dusted them carefully, checked to make certain nothing had been left stuck between their pages, then inspected their bindings and found them in good order with no loose pages. I checked the hand-colored fly plates in the McCain to make sure they were in pristine condition and found they were, their colors still bright and lively. The original owner of this book obviously had taken very good care of it, and I wondered what chain of events had consigned it to an antique store shelf next to the likes of Nancy Drew mysteries and Reader's Digest Condensed Books.

The Forge book had a few signs of wear but also was in very good condition. After encasing each book in a protective transparent plastic cover, I wrote detailed descriptions of both and photographed them with a digital camera, then posted the photos and descriptions on the store's website along with my asking prices—$12,500 for the McCain, $750 for the Forge. Only after that did I turn my attention to the remaining books, just to make certain I hadn't overlooked any other rare volumes that might bring a decent price. Since it was a rainy day and there had been little traffic in the shop, Sebastian and Vivian joined in.

We sorted the books into several boxes, one for volumes that might have some resale value in the shop, another for books whose value would be checked on the Internet to see if they were worth keeping in the shop or listing on the website, and another for books that could be donated to nursing homes or other charities. But the largest was for worthless books destined for the dumpster in the alley.

As we sorted them I saw many books I knew—a copy of Philip Wylie's *Three to Be Read*, which I'd perused as a teenager, then a battered copy of *The Cannoneers Have Hairy Ears*, the diary of a World War I artillerist, which I hadn't seen in a long time. Inevitably there were many Reader's Digest Condensed Books, an Arthur Conan Doyle anthology, a small library of books by P. D. James and Agatha Christie, some old Nancy Drews well-thumbed by generations of prepubescent girls, a copy of the right-wing polemic *None Dare Call it Treason*, which I consigned immediately to the dumpster box, and dozens of other dusty volumes.

Near the bottom of one box I came across a copy of Sam Slaymaker's *Simplified Fly Fishing,* a paperback showing the unmistakable marks of long years of hard service. For a moment I considered adding it to the books destined for the dumpster, then decided to put it on sale in the store instead. After all, it was a book about fly fishing, and I simply couldn't bring myself to throw away such a book. Besides, even in its ragged condition it might fetch a few dollars.

It took nearly three hours to finish sorting the books, with only a couple of interruptions from walk-in customers who'd braved the cold rain falling outside. At the very bottom of the last box was a small stack of slim, unbound books, each with a dark blue cover and the words "My Diary" stamped on in gold italics. There were about a dozen books in all, bound together with a dark velvet band. I'd examined them cursorily when I first inspected the collection at the antique store and knew they were diaries kept by a young woman in the late years of the nineteenth century. I tried to persuade the antique shop owner to keep them, but she insisted all the books had to go, including the diaries. Now I picked them up and started to place them in the box bound for the dumpster when Sebastian reached out and barred the way. "Wait a minute," she said. "What are those?"

"Dairies, handwritten by a woman. Late nineteenth century." I opened the topmost volume and checked the date. "This one is dated 1898. I assume the others date backward from there."

"Let me see them," she said.

"Be my guest." I passed them over, and she placed them on the counter and began to page through the top volume.

With my knees popping and a few other joints protesting, I got to my feet, leaned over, and, with Vivian's help, hoisted the big box full of books bound for the dumpster. Vivian held the back door open for me as I staggered out into the alley, lifted the box onto the edge of the dumpster and dumped the books into their semifinal resting place. Then I returned to the shop, picked up the box of books destined for a nursing home, carried it outside, and put it in the back of my van. By the time I returned to the shop, Sebastian had gone, taking the stack of diaries with her. Then, since it was Friday and I'd already taught my morning class and had nothing more on my agenda, I decided to go home.

Saturday morning I got up, had breakfast, then sat down at my computer and checked my email. There, to my great satisfaction, I found an order for the McCain book. It was from Arthur Fletcher, an old customer of mine who lived in Rochester, and seemed to have unlimited funds at his disposal which he devoted to the purchase of rare old angling books. He never quibbled over the price, either, and the $12,500 for the McCain book was more than my little store sometimes grossed in a month. It's not often something happens to make your day when the day has just started, so that left me in a celebratory mood. I poured a glass of my favorite single-malt and turned on the Metropolitan Opera broadcast.

Another good thing: the opera was *Peter Grimes*, one of my favorites, and not just because of the music. Grimes was a fisherman, even if he didn't practice catch-and-release and had a very bad habit of killing his young apprentices. I sat back and listened to the first act, simultaneously savoring the scotch, then poured myself a second glass. Sometime early in the third act I fell asleep, and when I woke up the opera was over. After that I turned on the television and watched the Red Sox until I fell asleep again.

And that took care of Saturday.

Sunday, still in a good mood, I went fishing, driving to a state park where a short hike through the woods took me to a small but happy trout stream. It was regularly stocked with confused little rainbow trout from a state hatchery, most of them with short spans of survival, and few lived long enough to reach real sporting size. But I didn't care; I purely enjoyed catching them on little dry flies which I tried to drop carefully and softly into each nook or cranny of the current where I thought a confused trout might be sheltering. As often as not, I chose correctly and finally lost count of the number of pale little hatchery rainbows I returned to the stream.

Monday I taught my morning class where we had a lively discussion about Harry Plunket-Greene's fine book, *Where the Bright Waters Meet*, which I had assigned my students to read over the weekend. So I was still feeling in good humor when I stopped at the shop Monday afternoon, where I was confronted immediately by Ann Sebastian, standing behind the counter like a linebacker. "Finally!" she said in apparent exasperation as I entered the shop, then leaned under the counter, pulled out a shopping bag, and placed it on the counter. She reached inside and drew out the stack of diaries she had taken from me Saturday.

"So," I said, "are you finally ready to get rid of those old things?"

"Not on your life. You won't believe this, but these diaries are worth more than all the rest of the books you've got in this shop!"

"You're right, I don't believe it. What in the world are you talking about?"

She turned and pointed to the black-and-white enlarged photo behind the counter. "You know who those people are?"

"Of course I know who they are. I'm the one who put that photo there. You should know them, too. That's Theodore Gordon. The woman was his fishing companion, whose name has been lost to history."

"It's not lost anymore." She gestured toward the stack of books on the counter. "These are her diaries."

"You've got to be kidding. This must be some sort of scam."

"No it isn't. Her name was Evelyn Chase."

"Sure it was, and I'm Izaak Walton. You remember that guy who came in here one day and tried to sell me the secret love letters of Ernest Schwiebert? I didn't fall for that one and I'm not going to fall for this . . . this, whatever it is, either."

"Oh, yeah? Well, come see for yourself." She handed me the stack of diaries and said, "you paid for them, so I guess they're yours. Why don't you take them into the office back there and read them? That way you won't be bothered if any customers should come in, unlikely as that may be."

I thought of doing as she suggested, but it occurred to me that in the unlikely event she was telling the truth about the diaries, I wouldn't want to suffer her self-satisfaction, so instead I took them and left for home.

On the way I began thinking of everything I knew about Theodore Gordon, based mostly on books I'd read, the books that propelled Gordon to the front ranks of American fly fishing. I still had copies in the shop and on the shelves of my home library. Foremost, of course, was John McDonald's massive 775-page work, *The Complete Fly Fisherman*, which included nearly everything Gordon ever wrote, except perhaps his laundry and grocery lists. As soon as I got home I picked up my hefty copy and looked up the two paragraphs I remembered where Gordon described his woman fishing companion; it was in a letter he wrote in 1903, the only mention of her in all those 775 pages.

"Eight years ago," he had written, "a young lady was my fishing companion quite frequently, and although we had to tramp four or five miles to reach the best part of the river, she never became too tired to enjoy the sport. She wore a Tam O'Shanter, sweater, short jacket and skirts, with stout shoes and leggings, and waded, as I did, without waterproofs, which are only a nuisance in warm weather. The constant exercise prevents one from taking cold, care being taken not to lie about long enough at lunch time to become chilled, though there is little chance of that when the summer sun is high in the heavens.

"This girl soon learned to cast a fly quite well, in spite of the fact that her rod was a poor one. . . . She saw portions of a most beautiful trout stream never before visited by a woman, and had many interesting experiences. An involuntary bath was the only misfortune she experienced, and she did not suffer from that."

McDonald also wrote a later work, *Quill Gordon*, which added momentum to the growing Gordon legend, as did *Fishless Days, Angling Nights*, mostly an account of Gordon's life written by Sparse Grey Hackle, whose real name was Alfred Miller. The picture that emerged from these books was of a consumptive little man with a bit of a mean streak and rumored bad habits, plagued throughout his life by respiratory problems that forced him to take refuge in the outdoors—or perhaps that was merely an excuse he used to get away and go fishing.

But there was no question that he wrote engagingly and well and was a great fly tyer whose influence on the craft endures to this day. He spent the last years of his life living reclusively in the Catskills, coughing up blood and trying to scrape up a minimal living selling the flies he tied, until he died in 1915. He was rescued from obscurity a generation later by McDonald, Sparse Grey Hackle, and other writers, whose enthusiastic portrayal of Gordon made him seem like the patron saint of fly fishers, someone who never had to use waders because he could virtually walk on water.

But then, I remembered, there came a book by Paul Schullery, the first genuine historian to tackle Gordon. I returned to my bookcase and took out my copy of Schullery's *American Fly Fishing, A History*, and turned to the appropriate chapter. Gordon, Schullery had written, "has been given credit for, among other things, the invention of the streamer, the original study of angling entomology in America, introducing the dry fly to America, introducing the nymph to America, originating the American style of dry-fly tying, originating the American approach to imitation and being, finally, 'the father of modern American angling,'" although none of those things was exactly true. "He is unrivaled in his importance as a symbol, and he is rarely matched in his qualities as a writer and angling thinker," Schullery wrote. "But he has been unfairly jerked from his context by our half-century binge of admiration. We needed a Theodore Gordon to fill out the lore of American fly fishing. We were lucky, though, to find that he fit the bill so beautifully. He was in practically no sense the original we have given him credit for being, but he was still remarkable."

Well, that pretty well cut him down to size.

Of Gordon's mysterious girlfriend, Schullery said, "Fittingly, her name is lost, and she survives only in two old photographs of her and Gordon fishing together," one of which, of course, was the one on the wall behind the counter in my shop. "This woman completes the bittersweet image of the complete fly fisherman," Schullery said. "It is American fly fishing's loveliest story."

Which it may well be. But now, I thought, if Sebastian's opinion of the diaries was correct, the ending of that story might just be in my hands. What would it reveal? Were Gordon and this girl just fishing? Or was something else going on? Could they have been having an affair? Getting it on together in the streamside shrubbery? Given what they were wearing in that photo on the shop wall, it seemed a little unlikely; it looked as if it would have taken them half an hour just to get their clothes off and another half hour to get them on again afterward.

But what if that *was* what they were really doing? Carrying on in the brush while mayflies danced overhead? How would the public react if that's what the diaries revealed? Back in the 1890s everyone would have been scandalized. But what about today? How would the fly-fishing community react to the news that Theodore Gordon, supposed patron saint of American fly fishing, had been carrying on with a girl who might be young enough to be his daughter? Given the present state of public morality, such news might actually boost Gordon's esteem in the public eye. I could hardly wait to start reading and find out.

Then it occurred to me I should be ashamed of myself; a man of my reputation and rectitude shouldn't have such puerile thoughts. And I still hadn't even determined if Sebastian was correct and the diaries were genuine.

I replaced my books on their shelves, poured myself a scotch, and sat down with the diaries of Evelyn Chase.

The first thing I noticed was her lovely penmanship, an art form that has since sadly disappeared from the American scene. Even her misspelled words were examples of fine craftmanship. I also noted that she mostly wrote well and wrote long, filling her pages with accounts that seemed far too lavish given the triviality of the events she described. There was no mention of Theodore Gordon in the first volume of her diaries, or the second, or the third, and I began wondering if I'd fallen victim to my own imagination, or, worse yet, been made victim of a practical joke by Sebastian. If so, she'd never let me live it down, and the thought irritated me.

But at least I had read enough to begin forming an opinion about Miss Evelyn Chase and her frequently mentioned friend, Susan Breckinridge. They appeared to be the somewhat spoiled children of well-to-do parents who attended something called Mrs. Boynton's School for Young Women, where, as far as I could tell, the curriculum was mostly about proper etiquette, proper behavior, social dancing, the latest fashions, good conversational habits, and, above all, fierce protection of one's virtue, all aimed at preparing young women for their introduction to society.

Evelyn, however, also appeared to be an athletic girl—a fairly skilled archer, accomplished horsewoman and avid outdoor person who enjoyed hiking and even fished some, having been taught by her father, who gave her an old bamboo fly rod. I had to admit she sounded like a girl who might have gone tramping four or five miles at a time with Theodore Gordon.

Let's see. In that 1903 letter, Gordon said he fished with his mysterious female friend "eight years ago," so that would have been in 1895. The third volume of Evelyn's diary, which I had just finished reading, ended early in that year. This was beginning to look a little promising, and I was starting to get excited again. Where would Gordon have been then? McDonald's vast collection of Gordon's notes and letters were all from a later time, so I returned to my shelves, retrieved my copy of *Fishless Days* and turned to Sparse Grey Hackle's account of Gordon's somewhat nomadic life.

Gordon apparently had made something of a living dealing in stocks and bonds, but according to *Fishless Days,* by 1893 his "health and financial resources, and his customers' investments, had all pretty well failed. So he and his mother came north and for a while lived with the Spencers, who by then were in South Orange, New Jersey. Apparently Gordon worked from time to time in New York brokerage offices—his letters intimate as much—but whenever he could raise the funds he would disappear, a couple of months at a time, to fish the Pennsylvania and Catskill streams. When his money ran out he would go to his father's relatives, the Pecks, in Haverstraw, New York, and the senior Peck would give him a job of some sort to tide him over.

"About 1900 the rest of his health failed, and he went to live permanently with the Pecks, eventually having fly tying and sleeping quarters in a detached building where he could be alone. It will be noted that even then Gordon was tying flies for the market, at least to some extent. He probably learned the art in Pennsylvania."

I knew that last part was wrong. In one of his many letters quoted by McDonald, Gordon said he learned to tie flies when he lived in the South. But if the rest of Sparse Grey Hackle's somewhat indefinite account was accurate, Gordon must have met Evelyn Chase in Pennsylvania or New York, and their fishing experiences—or whatever sort of experiences they were—must have occurred in one of those places, or perhaps during one of Gordon's disappearances into the Catskills.

Maybe the diaries held the answer, so I put *Fishless Days* back on the shelf and picked up the fourth volume. The first few entries again were mostly just trivial girl stuff, however, and my disappointment grew as I continued reading.

Then I came to the entry dated Thursday, April 4, 1895. Evelyn was at Susan's home, where they were helping plan the latter's

forthcoming wedding, in which Evelyn was to be a bridesmaid. In her
beautiful hand, Evelyn had written:

*Susan was so excited I could not help but be envious of her. She spoke
constantly of her fiancé, Artemus Harrington, whom she affectionately
calls "Harry," about plans for their honeymoon and where they will
live and how many children they will have. I'd met Harry several times
and was somewhat mystified about what Susan saw in him, but it all
made me wish I had a man in my life, someone who could capture my
excitement as Harry had somehow captured hers.*

*Then we were suddenly interrupted by Mrs. Fitzpatrick, Susan's fam-
ily's housekeeper, who said a man was waiting at the door with a package
for Susan's father. Susan told her to show him in and she returned with a
small, dark-haired, almost delicate man with a neatly trimmed mustache.
He was dressed in what appeared to be a very well-cut dark wool suit
with matching cravat and carried a small box in one hand and a rather
battered hat in the other. The hat and his shoes, which were scuffed and
scratched, did not appear to match the remainder of his dress.*

*He introduced himself very politely as "Theodore Gordon" and
said he was there to deliver a box of trout flies to Susan's father,
who had ordered them. Susan apparently had been expecting them
because she excused herself to go get her purse that she might pay him.
Meanwhile, I asked if I might see the flies. "Of course," Mr. Gordon
said, and he opened the small box and handed it over. I could scarcely
believe the contents, a dozen cunning little creatures constructed of
feathers and fur and I know not what, as delicate and lovely as if
God himself had made them, all arranged in a pair of neat rows.
I don't remember what I said but it must have been complimentary
because Mr. Gordon smiled broadly and thanked me. Nor do I remember quite what made me do it, but the next thing I said was, "Will
you show me how to make these?"*

*To my surprise he looked instantly crestfallen. "It would be my
greatest pleasure if I could," he said, taking the box from my hand,*

"but I'm very sorry I cannot. You see, I tie these flies for sale, they help supplement my income. There is a great deal of competition in this business and so I must consider my methods trade secrets and I cannot show them to others. I do hope you understand."

I suppose I must have looked disappointed—I really would have liked to see how he made the flies—but what he said next took me quite by surprise. "However, I can do something even better. I can show you how the flies are used."

"You mean take me fishing?" I exclaimed.

"That's precisely what I mean. If you'd like to go, of course."

By then Susan was back in the room looking at me as if I'd lost my mind. She paid Mr. Gordon and bade him good day, but before leaving he managed to whisper that he would call for me Sunday after church and I promised to bring a pic-nic lunch. Afterward Susan asked if I had indeed lost my mind. "What on earth were you thinking?" she said. "You know nothing about this man, and neither do I. How could you do such a thing? Have you forgotten everything Mrs. Boynton tried to teach us?"

There was really nothing I could say except that I was lonely, and I could hardly say that. And I had noticed Mr. Gordon was barely as tall as I am, perhaps not even that tall, and if he had unprincipled motives I thought it quite likely I would be able to defend myself adequately. And after Susan's eruption, I was more determined than ever to go fishing Sunday afternoon.

So there it was, I thought. Her first meeting with Gordon. Sebastian hadn't been joking after all. Where would this lead? I poured myself another thimbleful of scotch and resumed reading.

The segment I'd just finished was dated Thursday, April 4, so the following Sunday would have been April 7. There was no entry for that date, so I turned the page and there it was, under Monday, April 8:

Mr. Gordon called for me after church yesterday and we went fishing. I wore the same clothing I always wear when hiking in the mountains or the

woods and took the fishing rod Father gave me. I noticed a look of disap-
proval on Mr. Gordon's face when he saw it, but he said nothing. I also
took a small hamper with some cheese, fruit and nuts for lunch, which
Mr. Gordon carried while carrying his own fishing rod in his other hand.

We tramped for what seemed like miles along a faint trail through
woods and underbrush until we reached a small, swift stream. I did
not think even to ask its name, but it was obviously well known to Mr.
Gordon. We came upon a place where there was a long, lovely pool with
a grassy open spot along the shore, and Mr. Gordon announced that this
was where we would begin fishing. But first, he said, he needed to teach
me how to cast a fly.

He positioned me along the shore, placed Father's fishing rod in my
right hand, then took station behind me and put his left arm around my
waist. For a moment I froze! No man had ever put his arm around my
waist before and I began to think Susan had been right to warn me of
this man's intentions. But then I realized he was being very gentle and
I began to enjoy his touch; it seemed almost to make me tingle. Then he
took my right arm in his hand and began describing the motions neces-
sary to get the fishing line moving in the air, moving my arm back and
forth as he spoke, and told me to use my left hand to keep tension on the
line, which I did, and soon the movements became familiar and the line
began going where I wanted it. After a few minutes he stepped back so
that I could continue casting by myself, occasionally offering a bit of
advice to correct some error he had detected, until finally he said, "Now
you're ready to fish."

He took one of his flies—one of the same beautiful little creations
he had shown me at Susan's—and tied it to the end of my line, or
"leader," as he called it. Then he explained that insects hatched in the
stream and were taken by trout under the water and sometimes even on
the surface itself, which he said was always the best way to take them
if it could be done. As he explained these things, he directed my atten-
tion to a small disturbance on the surface across the pool. "That was
the rise of a feeding trout," he said. "Here, I'll show you," He cast his

own line toward the spot and the fly dropped gently to the water, started downstream on the current, and then—in a flash!—a trout had it in its mouth and broke out of the stream in a tumbling leap. I clapped my hands as Mr. Gordon swiftly subdued the trout, brought it ashore and deposited it in the wicker creel he carried. "Now it's your turn," he said.

It took an hour or more, and I was beginning to feel a little discouraged, but finally a trout rose and took my fly and Father's old limber rod bent until I thought it would break as the fish struggled at the other end. With Mr. Gordon's soft-spoken advice I managed to bring it to my feet where he caught it in his hand and held it up for me to see. It was, I suppose, about a foot in length, its body the color of rich cream and speckled with red and brown spots. He said it was a "brown trout," and I thought—I still think—it was one of the most miraculous things I've ever seen.

The remainder of the entry described how the pair had eaten their "pic-nic" lunch and spent several more hours fishing, during which Evelyn caught another trout—a smaller one this time—and lost two others that were only briefly hooked. Her concluding line was

I love it! I can hardly wait to go fishing again.

Well, no hanky-panky there, I thought—though Evelyn did say she almost felt a "tingle."

She didn't have long to wait long before fishing again. I found this entry for Thursday, April 11:

Mr. Gordon called for me today and we went fishing again, this time to a different stream. It was much faster and noisier than the one we fished before and Mr. Gordon said it could be fished properly only by wading. That was a new experience for me. The water at first was frightfully cold, but I soon grew accustomed to it, and the rocks were very slippery, especially where the water was running fast. Several times Mr. Gordon reached out to steady me when I began to slip; his grasp was firm and strong but always gentle, and once again I found that I enjoyed his touch. Neither did I have any fear of his intentions; he seems the perfect, well-mannered gentleman.

The fishing in this stream was different; it was filled with what Mr. Gordon called "pockets" and in the fast water it was necessary to cast quickly and try to drop the fly in one of these in order to entice a fish. It was a while before I got into the rhythm of it and more than an hour before I caught my first fish. It was a small trout, perhaps eight inches in length, and very different from the "brown trout" I caught last Sunday; this one was exquisitely colored in dark blue and brilliant orange with small fins edged in white, and Mr. Gordon identified it as a "brook trout," or really a char, whatever that may be. He said brook trout were a native species that once inhabited nearly all our streams, but lately they have been largely displaced by the brown trout, which were imported from Europe.

We put in quite a day of it, pausing for a pic-nic lunch made quite miserable by clouds of vicious mosquitoes, then returning to the stream where I managed to catch four or five more of the gorgeous little brook trout. By day's end I was comfortably weary, my feet were almost numb and I was nursing a regular galaxy of mosquito bites, but on the whole I had greatly enjoyed the experience and felt I had made good progress in my quest to become an angler.

I thumbed through more pages of female trivia until I came to this entry for April 18:

By prior arrangement, Mr. Gordon came for me again today and we returned to the first river we had fished. The day was warm, there had been rain the previous day and the trail was muddy. I was startled by a snake, but Mr. Gordon assured me it was harmless. We also encountered some poison ivy, but I knew from my hiking experience what it was and we managed to avoid it. Still, it seemed a long and difficult trek before we reached the stream.

Mr. Gordon immediately grew excited. "Look," he said, "there's a very good hatch in progress. We should do well today." I asked what he meant and he pointed to the numerous small flies that seemed to be hovering everywhere. "These are mayflies," he said, "the insects my fly patterns are meant to imitate." He described how the immature flies go through what he said was a "meta-morfosis," or some word that sounded like that, which only confused me, but he added that the immature flies then make their way to the surface, hatch out, dry their wings and take flight, unless they are first eaten by a trout, although, once in the air, many also are eaten by birds.

The flies seemed to be everywhere and my first instinct was to brush them away, as I would a mosquito, but Mr. Gordon said they did not bite; in fact, he said, they were the most graceful and gentle of insects. He proved the point by enticing one to land upon his finger, which he then showed me, and I could see it was a very fragile-looking, delicate thing, actually quite beautiful in its own way, and it did closely resemble one of Mr. Gordon's fly patterns. He tied one of the latter to my leader and one to his and we went fishing.

Trout were rising to the flies almost without inhibition and for several hours we enjoyed what Mr. Gordon called "great sport." He landed many more fish than I but I caught five, including two that were larger than any I had caught before. It was past 2 O'clock when the "hatch" finally ended and we had a late pic-nic lunch at the same grassy place where he first showed me how to cast.

Until then we had not spoken much, each of us being so intent upon our fishing, but as we relaxed I tried to strike up a conversation with Mr. Gordon, anxious as I was to learn a little more about him. Somewhat to my surprise, he seemed reluctant to speak about himself, answering most of my inquiries in the most general terms or in a mumbling fashion which I could barely understand. Eventually I gave up the task, resigning myself to the fact that he seemed to be a very private person and was determined to remain that way. But for that, however, it was a very satisfying day and I think I enjoyed the fishing the most I have yet.

Four days later, Monday, April 22, they were back on the water again.
This time, however, there was no hatch and the fishing was tough.
After a near-fishless morning, they settled down for lunch again in
a shady glen near the stream where Evelyn made another attempt to
find out a little more about Mr. Gordon.

He was as reticent as before, she wrote, *but based upon some of
the vague things he said I slowly came to the realization that Mr.
Gordon is living in near poverty and his only apparent income is the
meager sum he receives from sale of the flies he ties. That, in turn,
made me realize the time he has spent with me on the stream could
represent a significant financial sacrifice on his part—he could have
spent it tying flies instead—and, as my Father always says, "time is
money." So then I bluntly asked Mr. Gordon if I could pay him for his
fishing lessons.*

*"It's very kind of you to ask," he said, "but I enjoy our times together
on the stream and would never think of charging for the 'lessons,' as you
call them; I only hope you find them as satisfying as I do." And that
was where we left the matter.*

*But that evening, after Father came home, he suddenly asked about
what he called my "relationship" with Mr. Gordon. He said he had
made inquiries and some of the things he had learned were not favorable. "To begin with," he said, "your Mr. Gordon is a good twenty
years older than you are, a much older man than you should properly be
spending time with. Not only that, but he has apparently been unable
to sustain any sort of meaningful career and is obviously not a man of
good prospects. I don't think you should see him anymore."*

*Of course I protested I was not "seeing" Mr. Gordon in the sense
that Father meant, that he was only giving me fishing lessons which I
enjoyed. Nevertheless, he told me he did not want me to go with him
anymore. "You're still a very young woman with no experience in mat-
ters such as this and you can have no idea what Mr. Gordon's intentions
really are," he said. "Even if they are honorable, which I find doubtful,*

just seeing you in his company is bound to reflect unfavorably on your reputation, and our family's reputation as well."

"So are you ordering me not to go with him anymore?" I asked.

"I choose not to put it in those terms," he said. "Rather, I am asking you to use good judgment, for if you do that, I think you will conclude for yourself that you should not go with him anymore."

And that is where we left the matter, though I went to bed feeling quite upset about the whole thing.

Well. It began to seem as if the Gordon-Chase relationship was destined to be short-lived. I felt as if I were reading the script of a soap opera, though I could hardly wait to see what happened next.

What happened next was that, without commenting in her diary about her motivations or reasoning, Evelyn went fishing with Gordon again on April 29. She had little to say about the fishing—"just a few small trout," she told her diary—but much to say about Gordon:

Thinking about what Father told me, I tried again to draw out Mr. Gordon while we were eating our lunch, but he seemed as evasive as usual and I learned nothing new. For the remainder of the afternoon my thoughts were all on him and not the fishing, and I missed several rising trout as a result. "You're not paying attention," Mr. Gordon shouted from across the stream, a little harshly, I thought. It occurred to me then that in all the time we had spent together, Mr. Gordon had spoken of nothing but fishing and flies. He seemed obsessed with both and apparently uninterested in anything else. Certainly he had said nothing to indicate he might have any interest in me, except as a casual fishing partner and the usual provider of our pic-nic lunch. Could it be that fishing was his whole life? That nothing else mattered to him?

I had grown to love fishing, thanks largely to Mr. Gordon, but it is only one of many things I like. As for Mr. Gordon, I could not remember if even once he had called me by my name—I wondered if he even remembered it?—and here I was, a month after we had been fishing together, still calling him Mr. Gordon. It almost seemed like ours was more of a business relationship than a companionship.

I thought of the day I met Mr. Gordon, of how jealous I'd been of Susan and how lonely it had made me feel, and realized I still felt just as lonely. Perhaps Father was right; maybe my own judgment was beginning to tell me it had been a mistake to place myself in Mr. Gordon's hands. I did not think his motives were dishonorable, as Father evidently did, but I was beginning to wonder if he HAD any motives, and somehow that seemed just as bad.

With that cryptic thought, she closed the entry.

The diaries related that they fished together several times thereafter, though never as often as before, and Evelyn's entries grew brief, reporting little more than numbers of fish caught and the changing conditions as spring gave way to summer, hatches declined and the rivers dropped. There was no further mention of her father's desire for her to stop spending time with Gordon nor of any more efforts on her part to learn more from Gordon himself.

I found myself turning the pages of her diaries at a quickening pace until it was suddenly fall in Evelyn's world and she was writing about the colorful foliage along the rivers and how the clutter of leaves on their riffled surfaces interfered with the fishing, especially when dry flies were being used, as they were less and less frequently. There was a final entry describing a cold, nearly fishless outing early in October, and then the Chase family left to spend the winter in Florida, with no further mention on Evelyn's part of "Mr. Gordon," except that she had left him with a perfunctory good-bye. If there ever had been a prospect of a meaningful relationship between them, apparently it had expired in Gordon's reticence.

But that seemed wrong. How could the discovery of this lost diary and identification of Gordon's woman friend turn out to be so disappointing? If this was all there was, what had gotten Sebastian so excited? Hoping there must be more to the story, I kept paging through the diaries, skimming the entries Evelyn had written in Florida. For the most part they were trivial, tedious, and boring, and I sensed she was bored when she wrote them. Several times she expressed the wish that she was back home pursuing brook and brown trout in the cold streams of her neighborhood, and I wished so, too.

Both our wishes finally came true. Evelyn's family returned home late in March and in her diary entry of April 3, 1896, she confided that she had sent Gordon a note to tell him she was home and ready to go fishing again, if he had a mind to do so. The reply came several days later, and on April 13 he called for her and they left together.

Of course I did not tell Father, she wrote at the end of the day, *and I knew Mother would say nothing; she always allows me to do as I please. But it was not a good day. It was cloudy and cool and we walked mostly in silence; Mr. Gordon did not even ask about my winter experiences in Florida. There were still patches of old snow in the shade of the woods along the trail, and when we reached the stream, which had been hardly more than a brook when I last saw it, it was running full and fast. Mr. Gordon said there would probably be no hatches—it was too early for them—and the fishing probably would be difficult. He was right on both counts.*

Nevertheless, we prepared to go fishing—I had to ask assistance tying the fly onto the end of the gut leader because I'd forgotten how to do it—but when ready we both waded out into the cold, fast river—it was now much more than a stream—and began to fish. I had difficulty keeping my feet in the swift current and I hadn't been fishing more than fifteen minutes when my right foot suddenly slipped out from under me on a slick rock and I fell full-length into the river. Mr. Gordon was instantly at my side; he assisted me to my feet and helped me get ashore, where he quickly removed his tweed jacket and put it around my shoulders. I was soaked through and through, my undergarments as well as my outer garments, and shivering from head to foot.

"We must get you home," Mr. Gordon said, but I quickly demurred; I didn't want him to think I was not a good sport, so I told him, "No, the day is just beginning, I have been without fishing a long time and I want to stay and fish." He attempted to argue but I simply shook my head, tried to compose myself and wring some of the water from my skirts, and then waded bravely back into the river, though I was still shivering.

What followed was perhaps the most miserable afternoon of my life. I never did get warm; even after the sun broke through the clouds and my outer garments began to dry my undergarments were still soaked and it was most uncomfortable to move. Meanwhile there was no sign of trout to distract me from my discomfort, but I remained determined to show Mr. Gordon that I was not about to allow a little soaking to quench my spirit, and so, with clenched teeth, I went through the motions of fishing even though there was no sign of trout. When it came time for lunch I ate standing up because it was too uncomfortable to sit down.

It seemed forever before that wet, miserable afternoon was over and we made our way back through the woods, where most of the old snow had now melted, and finally reached home. There Mr. Gordon asked me rather hesitantly if I would like to go fishing again, thinking, I'm sure, that I would reply in the negative, and I saw a brief look of surprise on his face when I answered that I most certainly did want to go and we made plans for the following week. Then I went inside and told Mrs. O'Hoolihan, our maid, to draw me a warm bath, and I luxuriated in it until it began to cool, then got out, put on a warm robe, and sat gratefully by the fire, where I stayed until it was nearly time for Father to come home. Only then did I get up and dress for supper.

They went again a week later and Evelyn penned the following report in her diary:

This time we found a hatch in progress, the first we had seen. It wasn't a great hatch, but there were enough flies on the water to bring an occasional trout to the surface. Together we made our way downstream to a pool we both liked to fish, but as we came upon it we saw a small boy, about eight years old, seated on the opposite bank. When he saw us coming he picked up a handful of rocks and threw them into the pool, right where the trout were rising. Mr. Gordon immediately erupted in anger and gave the boy a fierce tongue-lashing for disturbing the water we were about to fish. He called the boy a "little rat" and several other names I won't repeat, until the boy finally got up and ran into the woods. I was shocked; I'd never seen Mr. Gordon so angry, nor had I dreamed he could use such language. "That was really very unkind of you," I told Mr. Gordon.

"Well, the little brat did it deliberately. The little skunk. Now we'll have to find another place to fish."

We waded to a different spot and I saw a trout rise and tried hurriedly to cast but felt my fly catch something behind me. I turned and saw the fly caught on a branch alongside the stream. Mr. Gordon said he would get it, waded over and tried to remove it but he saw the gut leader was hopelessly tangled around the branch. I waited until he untangled the leader and told me it was OK, though it looked rather badly wrinkled to me. Of course, by then the trout I had seen rising was gone.

We fished on and Mr. Gordon caught a trout—he nearly always caught trout—but it was a while before I saw another rise and tried to cast to it only to once more feel the sickening feeling of my fly caught somewhere behind me. This time it was fairly high in a tree, beyond anyone's reach. I could see Mr. Gordon mumbling something to himself as he reeled in and waded ashore; I couldn't hear what he was saying but I had little doubt it was about me and that it wasn't favorable. When he got to shore, he pulled on my line until the gut leader broke, leaving the fly and most of the leader hanging in the tree. Then he produced a new leader, sat down, attached it, then put a new fly on the end of it. Finally he handed me my rod and told me I needed to start paying attention. "Your casting is terrible," he said. "It looks as if you've forgotten everything I taught you. Start paying attention!" His manner was curt and left me feeling so upset that afterwards I couldn't concentrate on fishing. I kept making mistakes, caught my fly in a shrub twice more and went to get it myself when Mr. Gordon made no move to do so.

When it came time for lunch we each ate in silence until it became somewhat awkward, and then Mr. Gordon, apparently in an effort to break the silence, took out a large fly I'd never seen before and began talking about it. "This is called a 'Bumblepuppy,'" he said. "Isn't it beautiful?" He went on to tell me about all its parts, how he had invented it, and how wonderfully effective it was on several different species of fish. Finally he asked what I thought of it and, still feeling out of sorts, I blurted out, "To tell you the truth, I think it's rather ugly." And as if that weren't bad enough, I added, "I think it's also a bit childish for a grown man to be using a name like Bumblepuppy."

He looked as if I had slapped his face, and I was momentarily shocked that I had said such hurtful things. Without another word, he put the fly away, took up his rod and headed back for the river. I picked up the remains of our lunch and followed suit.

The afternoon fishing was no better for me than it had been in the morning. I was still feeling upset, had difficulty concentrating and caught nothing. At one point I got ahead of Mr. Gordon, saw a trout rise and tried hurriedly to cast without looking back, and again experienced the dreadful feeling of my fly getting caught on something. Then it suddenly let go, and I heard an angry shout from Mr. Gordon. I looked around and saw him standing behind me with my fly caught in the left sleeve of his jacket. It had torn a large piece from the fabric before the leader broke and now the piece of fabric and the broken leader were hanging from his sleeve.

"You clumsy _____!" he shouted, using a terrible word I had never before heard spoken aloud. It made my ears burn and hurt me to the

*quick, and without even thinking I reeled in my line and what remained
of my leader, waded ashore, gathered up the lunch hamper and headed
for the trail.*

"Where are you going?" Mr. Gordon called.

"Home," I said.

"Wait, I'll come with you."

*"No, I don't want you to come with me." And I started down the
trail.*

*I had not gone far before I sensed that Mr. Gordon was following. I
looked back and saw he was only about ten feet behind. And that was
how we went, a silent caravan of two trekking through the deserted
woods. It seemed almost eerie and for the first time since I had been
going fishing with Mr. Gordon I was beginning to feel a little fearful;
what would I do if he accosted me? Then I remembered there was a
bottle of sarsaparilla in the lunch hamper—I could feel its weight—
and if I had to I could swing the whole hamper at him, hard enough to
knock his mustache off, although I desperately hoped it wouldn't come
to that.*

*Fortunately, it didn't, and we went the whole way in tandem and in
silence, with him always following within ten feet of me until at last we
arrived at home—oh, how relieved I was to see it! I climbed to the top
step and turned to confront Mr. Gordon, who by then was standing at the
bottom step, looking like a crestfallen little boy, then spoke the words I had
been rehearsing silently in my mind the whole way home: "Mr. Gordon, I
think it best if we do not see one another again. Good-bye, Sir!"*

*I didn't wait for his reaction. Instead, I went inside to my room, sat
down and started to cry. I'm still not certain why I cried; I suppose it
was partly from disappointment—Mr. Gordon was my only male companion and I'd hoped our friendship might develop into something more
than it had. It also might have been partly from relief; Father had been
right, and I should have followed his advice. Mr. Gordon was obviously
not a man of good prospects.*

Still, I knew I would miss him.

That was all.

I paged rapidly through the remaining diaries hoping there would be more, but there was no further mention of Gordon. Evelyn did go fishing twice more, once by herself and once with a young man she had met at some social gathering, a young man who seemed to be developing an interest in her even as she began to reciprocate. But then, without explanation, in the fall of 1898 the diary abruptly ended, and the rest of Evelyn Chase's story was as lost to history as her name had once been.

To say I was greatly disappointed would be a monumental understatement. I'd thought I had the full story of Gordon and his girlfriend in my hands, a story that would turn the world of fly fishing on its head, but obviously that was not the case. It didn't even shed much new light on Gordon, if any; it simply revealed him as a rather one-dimensional person, a socially maladjusted man so obsessed with fishing he failed to see what the birds and the bees were doing. To be sure, his fly-fishing writings disclosed a personal charm that was otherwise hidden within his reclusive personality, but everyone already knew that.

As I thought about all this it occurred to me that I might just as well have been thinking about myself because in many ways I was rather like Gordon, a man who devoted his life to fly fishing and writing or talking about it, never married, and whose two women employees could scarcely be called friends. Surely there would be no John McDonald or Sparse Grey Hackle to sing my praises in the future, and the world would little note nor long remember Andrew Royster.

So who was I to judge Theodore Gordon or his peculiarities?

Those thoughts were so depressing I started again to reach for the scotch. I had so hoped the diaries would give me an opportunity to carve my own little footnote in the annals of fly-fishing literature, a small place among the crowded shelves of the masters whose works I'd read and taught and bought and sold. Might there still be a possibility of that? The diaries might not reveal anything about Gordon that wasn't already well known, but they *did* reveal the identity of

Evelyn Chase, and that was still important. It might even be priceless, and I, and Ann Sebastian, were the only ones who knew about it. If it leaked, its value would be diminished or destroyed, so I needed to keep it a secret—and make sure she did, too—until I could figure out the best way to make it public. Depending on how I did that, I might still be able to achieve a minor claim to fly-fishing fame; maybe even arrange some welcome financial compensation.

So what to do? I knew the professional thing to do—what my department chairman and my few academic colleagues would expect me to do, and what I would expect of them if the situation were reversed: Write a stuffy piece for some scholarly history publication that would probably be read by very few people and end up gathering dust in remote libraries. I'd be lucky to get $100 for the story, if I got anything at all.

But professors are expected to publish, so at least I'd get credit for doing that. For whatever that might be worth.

I knew that's what I *should* do. But the more I thought about it, the less appealing it seemed. Here I had the solution to one of fly fishing's oldest and deepest mysteries, and if I consigned it to some obscure academic publication, the fly-fishing world might never even hear of it. Besides, it was a story with high potential commercial value, worth lots more than a hundred bucks if published by the right source. It could do wonders for my savings account and, given my age and length of time to retirement, that ought to be an important consideration.

I studied the amber liquid in my glass as if it were a crystal ball that might hold the answer. In a sense it did; it made me realize my favorite brand of single-malt was getting quite expensive, and if I wanted to continue drinking it in retirement—which I certainly did—a little more income would be vital to my continued satisfaction.

And there was something else to consider: If the story appeared in a mass-circulation magazine or similar forum, then the name of Andrew Royster might finally occupy a small but permanent niche in the long, celebrated literature of fly fishing. That notion was greatly appealing.

I finished the scotch, neglected to brush my teeth so I wouldn't spoil the pleasing after-taste, and crawled into bed, with my mind pretty well settled on what I would do.

But I'd also have to do something to make sure Ann Sebastian kept silent.

After a mostly sleepless night during which I thought of little else, I arose to greet Tuesday morning with firm resolve to write a letter to the editor of *Upstream* magazine, which seemed to be the only surviving general-circulation fly-fishing magazine remaining after years of decline in that business. It also posted copies of most of its articles on its website, which might have as much circulation as the magazine, maybe more; that would disseminate the story of Evelyn Chase and the name of Andrew Royster to an even greater audience.

I had written several things for them in the past, and the editor, Mike Monahan, was familiar with my work. But it had been several years since my last article and I'd noticed with growing displeasure that the magazine had recently been moving in a different direction, away from any mention of fly-fishing literature or history and more toward trivial things like strike indicators, fishing tournaments, records, and other foolishness that actually eroded the foundations of the sport instead of enhancing them.

But surely they couldn't pass up a story of this magnitude—the solution to fly fishing's greatest mystery.

I decided to ask a $10,000 fee. That, I knew, would give Monahan pause, but I could also offer him exclusive publication rights; that should make the proposition more attractive. Maybe I could also offer him the book rights.

How could he resist?

After a quick breakfast I decided to check my email before heading to the university. The in-box had only one entry—from Ann Sebastian.

Oh-oh. It was very unusual for her to email me at home. With some trepidation, I opened it. There was no salutation—she never used one—just a brief message: "I thought you'd like to know that yesterday I sold that first-edition signed copy of Haig-Brown's *Fisherman's Winter* that we've had on the shelf for so long. A walk-in bought it with his credit card for $200."

That was all, except I knew it wasn't all; it was Sebastian's sneaky way of asking if I'd read the diaries. If I answered by email, maybe I could escape having to endure her self-satisfaction in person, so I clicked on "reply" and wrote the following:

"Thanks for the good news about the Haig-Brown; it's about time we sold that one. And yes, I did read the diaries over the weekend. You were right; they are quite a find. However, I need some time to consider how to proceed with them. Meanwhile, I'm sure I needn't tell you, but please keep this strictly under wraps, just between the two of us; if any word of it leaks out, it could and very likely would diminish or destroy the value of the discovery.

"I'll probably be in tomorrow—A."

I should have logged off at that point, but I waited a moment to see if she would send a reply, although I hoped she wouldn't.

But she did: "While you're thinking about how to proceed, I think you should also think about giving me a raise."

That was all, but it was enough to make me angry. I shut down the computer and left for my morning class.

The class was a disaster. I was so distracted thinking about the diaries and Sebastian's demand for a raise that I kept losing my train of thought and stumbled through my lecture, and most of my students grew bored and restless. I even spied one paging through a comic book he thought I couldn't see. It was a long hour for all of us.

Later, back in my office, I sat down at the computer and began composing a letter to Mike Monahan. I worked on it all afternoon, making several false starts and do-overs, then editing and re-editing until I finally ended up with what I thought was a good version:

Mike Monahan, Editor
Upstream Magazine
Mail Stop 54C31
Boulder, CO 80311

Dear Mike:

I am sending you this letter instead of an email because I have a story I believe is of such singular importance that I can't trust it to the doubtful security of email. I have in my possession a collection of diaries written by a young woman in the 1890s that reveal beyond any doubt she was the mysterious woman friend of Theodore Gordon, whose name was previously lost to history. I'm sure you and your readers are familiar with the famous photograph of Gordon and the unidentified woman fishing together, and the letter he wrote (published in *The Complete Fly Fisherman*) describing her as his frequent fishing companion.

I am prepared to provide you a detailed story revealing her identity and background along with excerpts from her diaries describing her fishing adventures with Gordon and the nature of their relationship. I hardly need point out the importance of this story; it will change much of what we know about Gordon's personality, his fishing practices, the obsessive secrecy of his fly-tying methods, and much more. I think it is no exaggeration to say that it will turn the fly-fishing community on its head.

No part of this story will be revealed before its publication in *Upstream,* and your magazine will have exclusive publication rights. Given that, and the enormous importance of the story, I feel justified in asking you to reserve more space than usual in the magazine, say at least 3,000 words. I also feel justified in asking for more than your usual fee. In this case, I believe a fee of $10,000 would be appropriate—indeed, for a story of this importance, I think it would be a bargain.

Thank you for your consideration and I will be looking forward to your early reply.

Sincerely.
Andrew Royster

OK, so maybe I did exaggerate a little, but I thought it was necessary to make sure I got Monahan's attention. I sent the letter using the return address of the bookshop, thinking that might add a little cachet.

After that the days and weeks dragged. I knew from experience that *Upstream*, like most magazines, was slow to answer queries, but thought maybe, for a story as important as this one, they'd answer in a hurry. No such luck.

While waiting, I scheduled my visits to the bookshop on Thursdays or Fridays when Vivian was minding the store, mainly so I wouldn't have to deal with Sebastian and her request for a raise. She soon figured out what I was doing, however, and was waiting for me when I stopped by one Thursday afternoon.

"Well, what about it?" were her first words.

"What about what?"

"My raise."

"Oh, yes," I said, as if it were a matter of very small importance. "I'll take it under advisement."

"Bullshit. I want an answer."

I'd never heard Sebastian use a word like that. This was serious; I had to tell her something. So I told her the first thing that came to my mind: "I've written to a magazine proposing a story about Evelyn Chase and I hope they will pay well. I'm still waiting to hear from them. If they come through with a good fee, then maybe we can work something out. Meanwhile, I have to ask your patience."

She gave me a sharp look. "OK," she said finally, "but I'm not going to let you forget."

"I know you won't."

After that we waited another week with no word. Then, the following Tuesday, Sebastian emailed me at home before I was ready to leave for class. "The mail just came," she said, "and there's a letter addressed to you from *Upstream* magazine. Is that the one you've been waiting for?"

"Yes," I replied. "I'll stop by this afternoon."

Which I could hardly wait to do. Sebastian was waiting behind the counter and, without a word, handed me the envelope. I opened it immediately and began reading:

Mr. Andrew Royster
Hooked on Books
241 Bradley St.
Boston MA 02116

Dear Professor Royster:

Thank you very much for your inquiry proposing a story about the identity of Theodore Gordon's woman fishing companion. I must say it triggered a lively discussion among our editorial staff, which led us finally to the conclusion that the fly-fishing community's interest in Gordon reached its peak in the 1960s and '70s and has now declined to a low level. In fact, many if not most of the current younger generation of fly fishers—which includes a large portion of our circulation—have hardly any idea who he was. Our modern readers are more interested in the improving technology of fly fishing or in traveling to new or exotic fishing destinations.

For those reasons we do not believe the story you propose merits the allocation of extra space or the large fee that you suggest. However, having said that, if you are willing to provide the story at our regular maximum length (1,500 words) and regular fee ($400), we would be interested in seeing it. With that in mind, we'll look forward to hearing from you again.

Sincerely,
Mike Monahan
Editor

I said the first word that came into my mind, a word I had very seldom used in my lifetime. It was a four-letter word, and it wasn't fish. Then I balled up the letter and angrily threw it partway across the room.

Sebastian picked it up, straightened it out, and read it. "Oh, my!" she said. "I'm so sorry. I know how much this meant to you."

I was too upset to speak. I just shook my head.

Sebastian came closer and spoke in what was, for her, an unusually soft voice. "Does this mean I won't get a raise?"

That hit me wrong. "My God, woman, how can you talk about a raise at a time like this? Can't you see this is a disaster? I just lost ten thousand dollars! What do you suppose that means for your raise?"

She edged forward until she was right in my face. "I'll tell you what it means," she said, her voice almost a whisper. "I just happened to make copies of those diaries the weekend I had them. I know a couple of women's magazines I think would be very interested, and I'll publish them myself if you don't give me that raise."

"You're trying to blackmail me!"

"You're bloody right I am."

We stood in silence for a long, sizzling moment, hostile eyes locked on one another, until at last I felt the anger start draining out of me, leaving only a feeling of vast disappointment. "All right," I said at last. "There's no need for this. I was going to give you a raise anyway."

"Sure you were," she said sarcastically.

"No, I mean it. You've earned it. You've done very good work for me, and I appreciate it. It won't be easy, but somehow I'll find the money for it."

She looked at me, her eyes no longer hostile. "Mr. Royster," she said, "I do believe that's the first time you've complimented me during the five years I've worked here."

"Can that possibly be true? If so, I must be losing my touch. Now I'm going home, and I think I'll get drunk."

And that's what I did.

In the end, I finally gave Sebastian a raise of thirty dollars a week, which seemed to pacify her. But I realized that if I gave her one, I'd have to give Vivian one, too, so I gave her a twenty-dollar-a-week raise. That put a serious crimp in the store's operating margin, which always had been close to the bone, so I had to make up for it by raising the price for some books and take on others I wouldn't otherwise have permitted in the shop (although I drew the line on adding books about fruits, vegetables, or Eastern religions). Those measures helped but did not quite make up for the deficit, which necessarily had to come from the shop's very slim profits.

I never seriously thought about doing a shorter article for *Upstream*, especially at the pittance they were offering, but I did finally submit a scholarly, dull, heavily footnoted version of the Evelyn Chase story to an obscure academic publication called *The Quarterly Journal of Evolving History*, which I knew was circulated mostly to university libraries, where it would end up unread until it landed in the recycling bin. Not surprisingly, the story wasn't picked up by any newspaper, magazine, wire service, or website, and as far as the fly-fishing world is concerned, the identity of Theodore Gordon's female fishing companion remains unknown.

But I did make sure my department chairman saw the article. I expected praise, but all he said was, "It's about time you published something."

That left me feeling about as low as I'd ever felt. I went home and tried to nurse my bruised ego with some scotch, but this time it didn't work. Eventually I realized the only hope I had of restoring my spirits was to go fishing, so I dipped dangerously into my slim bank account, got on the phone and put down a deposit for four nights at an inn I knew in the Catskills, one with access to some good private water. Then I emailed Sabastian and told her she was in charge of the shop while I was away, packed hurriedly and started on my way, anxious to start fishing and soothe my tortured soul.

Who knows? Maybe I'll even meet a young woman who wants to learn how to fish.

THE MAN IN BLACK WADERS

ELLEN HOFFMAN entered my cubicle unannounced, settled her considerable self into the chair in front of my desk, and slapped a thin manila folder on the desktop. She didn't say "Good morning" or "How are you today" or anything like that; it wasn't her nature. Instead, she said, "Do you know anything about fly fishing?"

That was Ellen; she'd spent most of her life working with words and seemed to have few remaining for her own use.

I pivoted away from my computer monitor, where I'd been playing a surreptitious game of solitaire, and answered "No."

"Well, you're going to have to learn damned quick. This is your new assignment." She pushed the folder toward me, hoisted herself out of the chair and departed.

As founder, editor and publisher of *On Trial* magazine, Ellen is my boss. She spent most of her sixty-some years working for half a dozen newspapers around the country until finally settling in New York and starting the magazine, which publishes stories about unusual criminal or civil trials that somehow escape the notice of other media.

My résumé, what there is of it, includes service as a reporter at four medium-sized struggling Midwestern newspapers, each trying desperately to survive while watching most of its advertising revenue flee to the Internet. As a junior staff member at each paper, I was among the first to go when layoffs were announced, even though I was convinced that I, Nicholas Kane, was ultimately destined for the roster of Pulitzer Prize winners. But after my fourth consecutive lay-off, I was seriously thinking of a new career, maybe flipping burgers.

Then Ellen came to my rescue. She had been managing editor at one of the papers where I spent my apprenticeship in poverty, and when she heard I'd been cut loose again she offered me a job at *On Trial*. She even offered a salary that allowed me to live in New York City, if only just barely above the poverty line.

During her long newspaper career, Ellen had developed a network of acquaintances and friends all over the country. Now she relied on them to send her tips about unusual trials taking place in their neighborhoods, paying for the ones that panned out, and I supposed the thin folder on my desk contained another such tip—maybe my path to a Pulitzer.

Or maybe not. I opened the folder to find a single sheet of paper with the text of an email printed on it. "Hi Ellen," it said. "I was on my way back from the coast last weekend when I stopped for the night at a little town called Wetside in the wilds of southwest Oregon. During dinner I overheard a conversation at the next table about an unusual trial that will take place here starting October 10. I went to the courthouse next day to make certain what I heard was the real deal, and it is. A local resident named Mickey Cutter is suing a man named Clint Steele, accusing him of—get this—plagiarism!

"Cutter is a retired teacher and high-school basketball coach who spends most of his time fly fishing the Biscuit River (don't ask me how it got that name), which runs through Wetside. Four years ago he published a book, *Fly Fishing the Biscuit*, based on his years of experience on the river. Last year Steele, who lives in Spokane, published a book titled *Eight Great Western Steelhead Rivers*, including a chapter on the Biscuit, and Cutter's suit accuses Steele of copying much of that chapter from Cutter's book. The suit seeks actual damages to be determined at trial and punitive damages of $250,000.

"The fact that the suit is over plagiarism is unusual in itself, but it also turns out that Steele is just about the most famous fly fisherman in the United States, maybe the world. He's written nine books, appeared in numerous fly-fishing videos, hosted two network TV fishing shows, is on the masthead of several fly-fishing magazines, and spends the off-season traveling around the country appearing at fly-fishing shows and conventions. His name is a household word among fly fishers and now his entire reputation is at stake. If he loses this trial it will all come crashing down—a 7.5-magnitude earthquake in the fly-fishing world.

"Wetside is too small to have a newspaper, and I did some checking on the Internet and found nothing about this case in any other Oregon papers, so if this interests you I think it could be a great and exclusive story for *On Trial*. Hope you agree."

It was signed by somebody named "Dana V.," which could have been either a man or woman.

Hmmm. Today was September 28, which left me precious little time to learn all about fly fishing before the trial. But I couldn't imagine there would be that much to learn. After a moment's thought, I decided my quest for knowledge about fly fishing in general and Clint Steele in particular should begin with a look at Steele's website, if he had one.

He had one, all right, and it was big, with many levels—biography, lists of his books and videos, TV program and show schedules, hosted trips; personal fly patterns, signature tackle, accessories and clothing, and a page where you could order a personally autographed photograph of Steele.

Autographed photo? I clicked on that and found myself staring at the color image of a handsome man with a black mustache and matching hair slicked back and tied in a neat little bun. Prominent eyebrows, a straight nose, and a firm jaw completed the picture. He was kneeling at the edge of an unidentified stream, fishing rod at his side, cradling an obscenely large fish in his hands—a trout maybe? I didn't know. But the photo was carefully arranged so that a patch of blue sky appeared over his left shoulder, leaving room for an autograph. I could order one of these autographed shots for just $25.

Clint Steele, I thought, was not lacking ego.

His biography said he'd been born in Boise, Idaho, and grew up fishing a number of streams I'd never heard of. He went to college at Montana State and worked summers as a fly-fishing guide on a number of other streams I'd never heard of. He graduated with a degree in journalism and caught on as a "field editor" for a fly-fishing magazine I'd never heard of. Then came the first of his nine books, the first of his videos, the first of his TV appearances, and the first of his hosted trips, followed by many more of the same.

Besides the autographed photo, his website offered lots of things for sale, including his books and videos. The latter included instructional videos—*Fly Casting with Clint*—fishing videos—*Clint Steele on Trout* (or salmon, steelhead, striped bass, bluefish, tarpon, bonefish, permit, redfish, sailfish, etc.), and travel videos (*Christmas Island with Clint Steele, Kamchatka with Clint Steele, The Seychelles with Clint Steele*, plus Patagonia, Chile, New Zealand and Alaska, etc.). Or you could order one of his four original "famous" fly patterns—Clint's Nymph, Cold Steele, Black Prince, or Black Knight—mounted individually in a "handsome plastic case," or half a dozen of each pattern, all "guaranteed to catch fish."

Then there was his signature line of tackle, accessories, and clothing. Clint Steele signature fly rods came in many different lengths and weights as long as you ordered them in black. The lengths and weights made no sense to me. Clint Steele signature fly reels were offered in many sizes and capacities, also finished in black. Clint Steele signature waders could be had for both men and women in various sizes, also in black. Clint Steele signature wading shoes also were available, again in men's and women's sizes, and—guess what?—black. I knew nothing about the costs of such merchandise, but all the prices posted on the website looked high to me. Clint Steele apparently had a lucrative business.

But black waders? I'd never owned a pair of waders in my life, but as a reporter I'd seen them on people forced out of their homes by Midwestern floods and I couldn't remember ever seeing anybody wearing black. Khaki maybe, or brown, gray, or camouflage, but never black. Black must be Clint Steele's favorite color—or rather, lack of color.

On a hunch, I started searching for Steele on other websites and blogs. He was mentioned frequently and usually favorably, and I found myself concurring with the opinion expressed in the email from Dana—whoever she or he was—that Clint Steele was just about the biggest name in fly fishing. But I also found a couple of blogs that were somewhat critical of him and one that was downright hostile, possibly motivated by jealousy. Digging deeper, I found an unconfirmed report posted on a fly-fishing forum that Clint Steele was known to travel with a live mouse in his luggage, which he would set free in his hotel room, complain to the management, and end up spending the night in an upgraded room free of charge. The story was repeated, again without confirmation, on another forum.

I wondered if it were true. Who would do something like that? Only a world-class chiseler, in my opinion.

I kept looking, going to some websites I'd learned to use as a reporter that often revealed a good deal more personal information about an individual than he or she would likely want the rest of the world to know. On one of them I discovered the interesting fact that Clint Steele was not the famous fly fisher's real name; the name on his birth certificate was Melvin Blifl. Clint Steele, it seemed, was the fly-fishing equivalent of a stage name.

I found myself beginning to dislike Clint Steele, even though I'd never met him. But I knew I had to suppress that feeling; a reporter is supposed to maintain objectivity.

So I switched gears and went looking for Mickey Cutter on the Internet. He didn't have a website. In fact, the only entry I found was for his book, *Fly Fishing the Biscuit*, a softcover published four years earlier by the Pacific Ocean Press, or POP, a small regional house in Seattle. A brief "about the author" description said Cutter had been born and raised in Wetside, Oregon, graduated from Oregon State University, taught history and coached basketball at Wetside High School for nearly forty years, then retired to fish and write. That was all; there was no photo.

Since I would presumably be staying there for the duration of the trial, I went looking next for more information about Wetside. What little I found indicated it had once been a thriving logging town with a sizable population, but closure of the local sawmill a decade earlier had left it a mere shadow of its former self; the last census listed only 384 residents. It also once had an annual community celebration called the Rust Festival, but that had been abandoned six years earlier due to "lack of interest." Yet Wetside remained the county seat of Fremont County, which explained why the trial would be held there.

Or did it? Why would such a trial be held in such an out-of-the-way little place? The only reason I could think of is that somebody's lawyer—probably Steele's—wanted to keep it away from media attention, which it would undoubtedly receive if it were held in Spokane, where Steele lived. I supposed I'd find out when I got to Wetside.

I looked for data on the local climate and found a one-word answer: "Wet." I searched for local accommodations and found only a single entry, the Spruce Grove Motel. It had a website displaying a photo of a typical example of 1960s American motel architecture, a two-story structure with a dozen rooms on the downstairs level and another dozen upstairs. I wondered if they had ever been full.

Next I went looking for any information I could find about the pending trial and found none. Evidently Dana V. was right that it had attracted no notice. I tracked down the telephone number of the Fremont County clerk's office, noted it was only about 11 a.m. in Wetside, and dialed the number. The woman who answered consulted a calendar or docket and confirmed the trial was scheduled to begin at 9:30 a.m. Monday, October 10, with Judge Emmett Frost presiding. Without being asked, she added the information that Judge Frost was visiting from Multnomah County, "up around Portland."

"Why isn't the resident judge hearing the case?" I asked.

"He's a friend of the plaintiff, so he had to recuse himself."

Nothing like a trial in a small town.

I asked if she knew how long the trial was expected to last. "A week," she said. "But who knows? The lawyers are from out of town, so I don't know how long it'll take."

I thanked her and hung up.

I sent an email to Gladys, *On Trial* magazine's all-purpose secretary, asking her to make reservations for me on a flight to Portland, a car rental and an upstairs room for a week at the Spruce Grove Motel in Wetside. I'd learned from unhappy experience that it's always best to stay on the top floor of a motel; if you're on the ground floor you can be sure the room overhead will be full of kids jumping up and down on the beds, or a three-hundred-pounder repeatedly stomping his way to and from the bathroom.

"Wetside?" Gladys replied. "You've got to be kidding."

I sent another email assuring her I wasn't kidding. I knew she would have to ask Ellen's approval for the travel expenses and Ellen would confirm there was actually a place called Wetside.

That done, I decided I'd better get busy and start learning about fly fishing; I didn't have much time. Again searching online, I found Manhattan had several fly-fishing shops and one was within walking distance, so I shut down my overworked computer, put on my jacket, and headed for the street. I found the place after a ten-minute walk, went in, and looked around. A clerk saw me and came over immediately, asking if he could help.

"Uh, I'm just looking," I said. "I'm new to fly fishing; actually I'm just thinking of taking it up, so I thought I'd look around and see what I could learn."

"Well, feel free, and just holler if you have any questions," he said.

Not knowing where to start, I turned randomly into a section I quickly discerned was devoted to fly-making materials. I'd never seen anything like it. It looked as if the shop had plumage from all the world's birds and pelts from all its animals, a regular Noah's ark of packaged tufts, scraps, quills, and fibers, plus many synthetic materials with exotic names like Flashabou, Fettuccine Foam, and Sparkle Organza. There were spools of tinsel, wire, silk and thread, hooks of many shapes and sizes, some black, others silver and gold, some with barbs, some without. There was a display of complicated-looking fly-tying vises, bobbins, scissors and other tools whose purpose wasn't clear to me, along with bottles of fly-tying "dope," whatever that was. The shop atmosphere was rife with the faint but pervasive odor of mothballs.

Looking elsewhere, I found racks of rods and shelves of reels, displays of shirts, hats, caps and gloves, and lots of waders—none of them black. Most fascinating, though were the thousands of colorful flies, some looking real enough to spread their wings and rise from the small plastic compartments in which they were arranged. Some were so small they might have been imitation fruit flies, others so large and handsome they would have been suitable for framing, as indeed some of them already had been and were mounted on the wall. Many were so intricate and perfect they could only be considered works of art.

Here, before my eyes, was evidence of a large and thriving subculture of which I had been entirely unaware, a highly developed society with its own codes and jargon, its own customs and rituals, a colorful and complex world all to itself. I felt a total stranger trespassing on its premises, yet somehow I also felt strangely and strongly attracted to it.

I ended up staring at a display of fly-fishing books and videos—at least I understood what those were for—when the clerk caught up with me again. "This is our catalog," he said, handing me a thick, colorful, magazine-sized publication. "Everything you see here is in it and more besides. And there are instructions for ordering online, which you can do anytime. Or feel free to drop in anytime, and we'll be glad to help you with anything."

I thanked him and headed back toward the office, my head spinning and filled with doubts at how much I had to learn to fathom what this fly-fishing business was all about.

Back in my cubicle I thumbed through the catalog and found a page advertising fly-fishing schools offered by the shop. "These comprehensive weekend schools will teach you everything you need to know to get started in fly fishing," the catalog said—"casting, knots, fly selection, stream tactics, entomology, you name it."

That, I thought, is exactly what I need, so I picked up the phone, called the shop and asked if they had any schools scheduled before October 10. The clerk who answered—he might have been the same one who helped me in the shop—consulted a calendar and answered regretfully that they did not; the next class was not until the weekend after the 10th.

So much for that idea.

I tried to resume my fly-fishing education by looking at other websites. What I found wasn't very helpful; there were so many sites and they were so variable in content that I soon gave up. The only thing I learned was that fly fishing was a sport heavily laden with celebrities, of whom Clint Steele was the foremost. But I had known that already.

I decided my time might be spent more profitably at the public library, so that's where I went next. And that's where I learned that fly fishing has even more books—many more—than it has celebrities. There were also lots of videos, including "Fly Casting with Clint." I checked it out along with several promising books, including Steele's *Eight Great Western Steelhead Rivers* and another titled *Permit Me*,

which I subsequently learned was about fishing for a saltwater species called permit, which I'd never heard of. The library didn't have a
copy of Mickey Cutter's book, so I returned to my office and ordered
a copy from the Internet. Everything else I took back to my dingy,
cramped, hugely overpriced apartment to study.

And that's pretty much all I did for the next few days. Somewhat to
my surprise, I learned that fly fishing is a complex sport combining
elements of philosophy, nature study, literature, biology, limnology,
and probably a few other ologies I hadn't encountered. It even had
touches of religion.

Oddly enough, it was Steele's casting video that was most helpful.
I didn't like his high, nasal voice, but his presentation was clear and
well-organized. From it I learned that the fly rod acts as a lever to
propel the weight of a thick, tapered fly line, which has on its end a
translucent leader with a virtually weightless fly attached, and in this
it is different from all other forms of fishing where casts are made
with the weight of the lure pulling an almost weightless line behind
it. That made everything clear and helped me understand why there
were so many different lengths of fly rod and weights of fly line.

The video was much clearer and easier to absorb than Steele's
prose. I figured someone else had written the video script and Steele
had read it off a teleprompter.

When Cutter's book arrived I opened it and started reading the
foreword:

> Let me tell you about a river. Its name is the Biscuit—an odd
> name for a river, but that's not the river's fault. It was the
> name given by the country's original inhabitants in a language
> no longer spoken or understood. The earliest European set-
> tlers translated it phonetically into a word most often spelled
> "Boisquoit," or something similar. Inevitably, the word was
> eventually corrupted into an Anglo term more familiar to the
> settlers, and the name became Biscuit. The exact meaning of

the word has been lost to history, but there's an enduring legend that in the long-dead language of the local tribes it meant "thunderwater." That seems unlikely to me, because the Biscuit is, at most, a medium-sized river, and while it may sometimes run fast and noisy, never have I heard its sounds rise to the level of thunder. More likely this was the brainstorm of some real-estate developer.

The Biscuit is a rain-fed river, rising in coastal mountains where rain is abundant and frequent. Its headwaters are a series of small creeks that flow from the high country in shadowed canyons, creeks with names like Blaze, Spar, Harvey's, Bitter, Spruce, and Fog, and finally join one another to form a juvenile river that soon grows larger with the addition of other tributaries as it makes its way first south, then abruptly turns west to begin a sixty-mile flow to the sea.

Those little headwater creeks have been treated badly. A couple of generations of loggers cut them down to their edges and left them full of trash and silt washed down from the naked slopes. Miraculously, over time, most of those little streams managed to recover, and their recovery brought health back to the river itself. Of course it is not the same river the Indians knew, no longer as swift or cold or clear, and its runs of salmon and steelhead are no longer as great as they once were. But they are still good, especially the steelhead runs, and the Biscuit, although little known, provides steelhead fly fishing of a sort not found on most contemporary rivers, even those of much larger size.

There are two runs of steelhead in the Biscuit. The summer steelhead come first, usually about the time June becomes July. They trickle in steadily until late September, and although there never seem to be a great many of them, they spread quickly throughout the river and if you know where and how to look you can usually find them somewhere. The winter run is much larger and usually bursts into the river during the first big freshet of December. This vanguard is followed by a steady stream of latecomers, and they all join together and rest in the lower pools until mid-February, when the business of spawning begins. So during those seasons—July through September and December into February—the Biscuit offers fly-fishing opportunities worthy of pursuing.

I know this because for much of my life I have had the good fortune to live in a cottage next to the river, and whenever it was in fishing shape—and I was in similar shape—there were few days when I didn't spend at least a little time casting a fly into its tempting waters. Many other days I started fishing in the early dawn and continued until I could start counting stars in the evening sky. When you spend that much time on a river, you get to know it very well, to understand the idiosyncrasies of each pool and pocket, the ways and habits of the steelhead, the flies and tactics that seem to work best.

The fishing was never fast. Steelhead fly fishing never is. But if you have patience, persistence and the willingness to put up with some occasional mild discomfort, the results will nearly always prove well worth the effort. One of the most thrilling sights in angling is that of a summer steelhead rising spectacularly to a riffle-hitched fly on the surface, and the sudden hard take of an unseen winter fish is scarcely less exciting. If you think about it, there really aren't very many people who have experienced such moments. You're lucky if you are among the few who have.

If you haven't yet, maybe this little book will help you get there. In these pages I propose to tell you much of what I have learned about the river and its fish. I confess I approach this task with some trepidation, because some of these secrets were very hard-earned and I have a natural reluctance to share them. However, I was a teacher by profession (I'm retired now) and have always believed that anyone with knowledge is obligated to share it, else we fail to keep the human experiment moving forward. That's my motivation, just so you understand it.

But while I'm willing to share with you some of what I've learned, I'm also bound by conscience to ask your pledge to use the knowledge wisely, keeping the health of the river and its steelhead always in mind. By that I mean it's all right if you keep a fish now and then—remembering always that each one you keep may subtract many others from future runs—so long as you do it in strict moderation and with valid purpose. I mean also that you should become a champion of the fish and the river and be willing to fight for both, keeping the Biscuit and its tributaries free from again being logged down to their banks, or dammed, or filled with silt and trash, or becoming the victims of all the other mean and selfish things people to do rivers and their inhabitants.

Do I have your word that you will do this?

OK, then. Let's get started.

—Mickey Cutter

After reading that I found myself liking Mickey Cutter. It was obvious he wasn't a very experienced writer, but he had a natural flair for the language and a friendly manner that drew me in. I looked forward to meeting him and looked forward even more to covering the trial that would determine if Clint Steele had stolen some of Cutter's well-chosen words.

But I had to remember to be objective; as a reporter, I could not allow my liking for Cutter to influence my coverage of the trial.

Next I started comparing Cutter's work to Steele's chapter on fishing the Biscuit. Almost immediately I found similarities and outright duplications, which made me think Steele would be in for a tough time defending Cutter's lawsuit.

After another week or so of reading and cramming, my brain was so full of information about fly fishing, fly casting, fly tying, fly patterns, fish, knots, tactics, accessories, and nomenclature it seemed anything more might cause an aneurysm. I still wished I could actually take a fly rod in hand and have the experience of casting, hooking a fish and landing it, but my main goal was to understand the sport's terminology well enough to make sense of what I would hear during the trial, and I thought I had achieved that goal.

Now it was time to head for Oregon.

It was raining when we landed at Portland International Airport. After I collected my bag and checked out a rental car it was still raining. The clerk at the rental desk gave me a map that purported to show how to navigate Portland's tangled freeways and bridges until I reached southbound Interstate 5. The map made about as much sense as a diagram of the human digestive tract, but fortunately the rental car had a GPS system with a bored female voice that patiently issued instructions, which finally spit me out of town onto the soaked surface of I-5.

I hadn't driven since I moved to New York—I mean, what's the point?—so I got in the right lane and watched traffic in the other lanes speed past as if I were standing still, throwing up rooster tails of spray and water that cascaded over my windshield. The speed limit signs posted along the freeway apparently were minimums; the average speed of the other traffic was at least twenty miles an hour faster than I was going or wanted to go. Huge eighteen-wheelers zoomed past, sending up tsunamis in their wakes. I hunkered down in the driver's seat with the windshield wipers at high speed and listened carefully for my electronic escort to issue instructions.

For a long time she was silent. The freeway was straight as an arrow, and it would have been a boring drive if not for the potentially deadly conveyances hurtling past. Or if it hadn't been raining. The rain seemed to come in waves, sometimes a deluge and sometimes backing off to a heavy drizzle, but never ceasing altogether.

Then I suddenly heard the disembodied voice of my GPS escort advising me to "prepare to turn right in one mile." Sure enough, there was an exit ahead, and with a sigh of relief I left the nearly submerged interstate and turned onto a two-lane secondary road that led into a thick forest of second-, third-, or fourth-growth timber. It was getting late in the afternoon of what had been a dark day to begin with, and it was darker still in the narrow canyons between the trees.

I followed the road for what seemed an interminable length of time until my digital escort roused herself again and told me to turn left in one mile. Seconds later I came to a bridge and caught a glimpse of a sign that informed me I was crossing the Biscuit River, but it was too dark to see anything. Then I came to an intersection marked "River Road" and turned left as instructed. This road was even narrower than the one I had been on, so I slowed and turned on the rental car's high beams, sensing rather than seeing the river off to my left in the raining darkness. The road meandered through the forest in a series of twists and turns, perhaps following the invisible route of the river.

After about ten miles I came upon a bunch of signs warning that a sharp curve was ahead, so I slowed again and entered a nearly ninety-degree turn to the right, realizing that I was now traveling almost due west. Once again I sensed the river out there on my left in the darkness.

Time passed with the only sounds the monotonous stutter of rain on the windshield and the rapid swish of the wipers. Then my digital escort startled me again by suddenly rousing herself to tell me I was "arriving at my destination." Sure enough, on the side of the road was a metal sign that announced the outer limits of Wetside, Oregon. Beneath those words was the single word "Population." I assumed there had once been numbers after it, but the high beams showed they had been obliterated by several rusting bullet holes. Welcome to Wetside.

At first there was no other evidence of a town, but then in the distance I saw a red light on the side of the road. The light refracted through every raindrop on the windshield, making it appear as if I were driving into a shower of sparks, but the red droplets gradually resolved themselves into a neon sign and eventually I made out the words Spruce Grove Motel.

I pulled off the road into a gravel parking lot with several overflowing puddles, stopped, and surveyed the building in front of me. It was the same structure I'd seen in the website photo, except it looked older in the flesh. Three cars were parked in the lot, two near the office and one at the far end. The office itself had a carport-like drive-through, which I was glad to see; it meant I wouldn't have to get wet.

I stopped in the carport, got out and stretched, trying to rid myself of the stiffness that had set in after hours on the road, then went inside. It was typical of every motel office I've ever seen, with a counter stretching three-quarters of the way across the rear of the room, a small table on the left with a coffeemaker on it, a vending machine stocked with candy bars and soda pop on the right, and a huge vase containing a sad-looking plant. Behind the counter was a pudgy, balding man with his eyes locked on a small TV set. "Hep you?" he asked, looking up.

"I sure hope so. I have a reservation."

"You must be Mr. Kane."

"That's right." I approached the counter, got out my wallet and plunked down my driver's license and credit card. The proprietor, if that's what he was, scooted over—his swivel chair had casters—and pushed a registration card and ballpoint pen across the counter. I filled in the requested information while he ran my credit card and typed the information from my driver's license into a computer behind the counter. "You here for the trial?" he asked, glancing up again.

I wasn't anxious to have anybody know that, so I said, "Let's just say I'm here on business."

"Suit yourself." He pushed my license and credit card back across the counter and said, "I've got you in Room 17. That's on the second floor, as you requested." Then he rummaged in a drawer and withdrew a key with a big plastic tag attached that said "Room 17" on it. Evidently key cards had yet to make their debut in Wetside.

I pointed at his computer monitor. "Mind if I have a look at that?" I asked.

"Huh? What for?"

"I'd like to see who else is registered. I'm supposed to meet some friends and they might be staying here." It was a journalistic lie, so it didn't count.

"Sorry, but it's against policy."

I reached in my wallet again, withdrew a $20 bill and put it on the counter. "Still against policy?"

He looked eagerly at the $20 bill, then shook his head. "Can't allow it," he said.

I took out another $20, put it next to the first, then looked at him questioningly.

He stared at the money for a moment, then reached out, crumpled it in his hand, and put it in his pants pocket. Then he got up, muttered "Excuse me a minute, got to check on something," and headed into the back room.

The monitor was on a swivel, so I reached over the counter and turned it around where I could read it, then took a small notebook and ballpoint pen from my pocket. I saw a woman named Olivia Pine was in Room 5 on the first floor. She had given her address as Applegate & Fromm in Portland, which I assumed might be a law firm. Maybe she was Mickey Cutter's attorney.

Room 7 was occupied by Emmett Frost, the visiting judge from Multnomah County.

Room 11 was registered to somebody named Eric Gruen of Pittman, Bryce & Danvers, which I presumed was another law firm, this one in Spokane. Maybe Clint Steele's attorney?

Room 12 was occupied by Merritt Bryce from the same law firm. A partner, no less. Maybe Steele's law firm had sent a double team.

Room 24—the last one at the far end of the second floor—was registered to Clint Steele.

I jotted down the information and turned the monitor back around just as the proprietor shuffled back into the room. "Sorry about that," he said. "I think you're all set. Coffee here in the morning," He pointed to the coffeemaker.

"Anyplace I can get something to eat around here?"

"Sure. Just head up the road toward town and you'll see the Riverside Café on your right. That's about the only place and it's still open, except you could probably get a microwave pizza or bowl of popcorn at the Knothole Tavern. That's a block beyond the Riverside."

I thanked him, got in my car and drove out from under the overhang. Beyond the two cars parked nearby my headlights illuminated what appeared to be a black Suburban parked at the far end, the same vehicle the Secret Service uses to squire the president around. Through the rain I could barely make out what appeared to be the decal of a highly colored leaping trout on its driver's side door. Curious, I drove closer and confirmed that's what it was. Then I noticed several words under the decal, all in gold paint:

CLINT STEELE
Professional Fly Fisher

I wondered if the back end of the Suburban was stuffed with $25 autographed photos.

I turned around, parked my car beside the flight of steps next to the office, fetched my bag, and climbed to the second level balcony, which I was glad to see protected from the rain by an overhang. I opened the door to Room 17 with the key, stepped inside and felt for a light switch next to the door. When the light came on I was reminded instantly of a classic line from one of Ian Fleming's James Bond novels: "It was a room-shaped room with furniture-shaped furniture."

The centerpiece was a queen-sized bed with a noticeable swale in the middle that looked as if it would hold water if the roof leaked. Across from the foot of the bed was a three-drawer chest with a small television set on top—apparently wide-screen televisions also had yet to make it to Wetside. Same for Wi-Fi. There was a window in front with drapes over it. Next to it was a battered round wooden table with two battered wooden chairs. A small bed table held a telephone and a digital clock that was a couple of hours behind. A portable wooden wardrobe in the corner next to the bathroom entrance completed the ensemble. The wall above the bed had a couple of faded prints, one of a huge vase with irises sticking out of it, the other an apparent street scene from some run-down town in Italy. The whole place smelled of disinfectant.

I put my bag on the table, pulled back the stained coverlet on the bed, and checked the sheets for evidence of bedbugs or other creepy-crawlies, noting with satisfaction there did not appear to be any. Then I went in the bathroom and checked the tub, remembering my last assignment in a little east Texas town called Cotton Ball where I'd stayed in a bed-and-breakfast with a teeming population of cock-roaches, some nearly as large as candy bars. But there was nothing in the tub, either, thank goodness.

I left my bag on the table, still zipped tight so if any wildlife did come along it couldn't get inside. Then I left to explore Wetside and find some dinner.

Wetside turned out to be a one-street town, actually just a half-street town. All its buildings were on one side of the street, on my right. The high beams of the rental car penetrated the rain on the other side to reveal a narrow strip of grass with a pair of park benches fac-ing away into the darkness toward what I assumed was the Biscuit River. Past the Spruce Grove Motel the first structure was a well-lit service station with attached garage, and I wondered if it was the last place remaining in the western hemisphere where you could get both gas and mechanical assistance. Beyond the station were two dark, empty storefronts, a fire hall, and an unpaved side street leading inland, with the faint lights of a couple of houses gleaming dimly through the downpour.

Next was a small post office, then the Riverside Café, also well lighted, with eight or ten vehicles in its potholed parking lot. I figured that would be my destination, but I wanted to see the rest of the town first, so I kept going.

Just beyond the café was Mike's Market, still open with lights blazing and busy if the number of cars parked in front was any indication, then another side street similar to the first. On the corner was a small community chapel with lights on inside, and I remembered it was Sunday night; maybe there was a church supper going on.

Next came a hardware store, the Knothole Tavern, another empty storefront and another unpaved side street. I'd heard Oregon was on the cutting edge of the microbrew revolution, but the only neon signs in the Knothole Tavern's dirty windows advertised a couple of cheap industrial beers. Several beat-up, mud-spattered pickups were parked outside. I figured the Knothole Tavern looked like a good place to avoid.

I passed another side street, and my headlights picked out a huge, three-story, rain-streaked wooden structure on my right. There was just enough light to make out the words "Fremont County Courthouse" over the double doors. So this was where the trial was to begin tomorrow.

On the far side of the courthouse was a long, low wing with a one-word blue neon sign barely visible through the rain. It said "sheriff." Evidently this was where the local posse hung out.

Beyond that I could dimly see several larger buildings clustered together. A roadside sign advised these were the Wetside Public Schools. There was also a reader board with the information that Wetside High was "Home of the Fighting Otters." I supposed this was the high school where Mickey Cutter had taught.

I passed another side street that appeared to lead to a parking lot for school buses, then came to a field covered by a thick growth of blackberry vines and tall grass, topped by the surreal shapes of metal wreckage and rusting cable. Maybe this had been the site of the now-closed sawmill and the annual Rust Festival before its demise.

Beyond that was nothing but darkness, so I made a U-turn in the empty road and headed back to the Riverside Café. I found a place to park, dashed through the rain to the entrance and entered a scene that might have been from the 1950s. The café had a counter with padded stools, booths along the walls, and Formica-topped tables with chrome borders, and it was noisy with conversation and the clatter of pots, pans, and utensils. It also had a typical restaurant smell, a combination of cooking scents, both good and bad, that blended into something like brussels sprouts.

About half the tables and booths were occupied, so I slid into one of the unoccupied booths, which had place settings for four people. Almost immediately a rather pretty but tired-looking thirtysomething waitress descended upon me with a laminated menu in one hand and a pitcher of ice water in the other, which she poured into an empty glass. She wore a name tag that identified her as Jenny. "Tonight's special is pot roast with carrots and onions, mashed potatoes and gravy," she said. "Be right back," and away she went to another table.

The menu was pretty standard for almost any restaurant that counted long-haul truckers among its usual customers. There was chicken-fried steak with mashed potatoes and gravy, an open-faced steak sandwich, macaroni and cheese (with sausage extra), an assortment of burgers and sandwiches, fried chicken, and so on. But the pot roast sounded good, so when Jenny returned that's what I ordered. "Good choice," she said. "You want anything to drink?"

I'd heard Oregon was famous for its wines, so I turned over the menu to look for a wine list. I found it at the bottom of the menu. The choices were red, white, and pink. Evidently wine snobbery had yet to reach the Riverside Café. "I'll stick with the water," I said, and she headed for the kitchen to deliver my order.

The pot roast, when it came, was actually pretty good, much to my relief and satisfaction, so I paid the bill, left Jenny a nice tip, and headed back to the Spruce Grove Motel. This time there were four cars in the lot; another had been parked beside Clint Steele's Suburban at the far end of the ground floor, and I assumed the inhabitants of Rooms 11 and 12 had returned from dinner. Maybe they had been at the Riverside when I got there, but I wouldn't have known who they were.

I parked the rental car and climbed the stairway to the second floor. As I reached it I heard loud voices at the far end of the balcony and saw the door to Room 23 was open and a man who looked like the photos I'd seen of Clint Steele was just entering the room, though I remembered he had been registered in Room 24. But then he stopped and exchanged angry words with another man, who looked like the pudgy guy who'd checked me in. The pudgy guy turned away and Steele stepped into the room and slammed the door. The pudgy guy started walking my way and I saw he was indeed the guy who'd checked me in.

"Trouble?" I asked.

"Guy found a mouse in his room," he said gruffly.

"Uh-oh. What'd you do? Put him in a different room, on the house?"

He just grunted and walked on.

Well, that told me the legend of Clint Steele releasing a mouse in his room to get a free night's lodging was probably true after all. Of course, there was another possibility; given the age and condition of the Spruce Grove Motel, I thought it might have its indigenous mouse population.

Back in my room I took a quick shower, without any evidence of wildlife in the tub, and climbed into bed. It had been a very long day and I was weary. I settled myself in the middle of the swale—there was hardly any alternative—and quickly fell asleep, secure in the knowledge that nothing short of a magnitude 9 earthquake could make me fall out of that bed.

When I woke up next morning and looked outside it was raining. Big surprise. I dressed hurriedly, passed up the coffee at the motel office, got in the rental car and headed through the rain to the Riverside Café. I decided not to have the signature item on the breakfast menu—biscuits and gravy (Biscuit River, get it?)—and settled instead for French toast and sausage. Then I headed for the courthouse.

To my surprise, most of the parking spaces around the old building were filled with mud-stained, beat-up pickups or SUVs and I had trouble finding a spot. It was still raining, of course, so I made another dash through the narrow spaces between parked vehicles and amoeba-shaped puddles of inestimable depth, clutching my laptop computer under my jacket to keep it dry.

Once inside I found myself in a dark lobby with county offices on both sides and a pair of stairways at the rear, one on either side, converging on an upstairs balcony where a pair of double doors stood open to disclose a crowded courtroom. All the seats were filled and the overflow was lined up along the walls, which surprised me; surely there weren't that many people interested in the trial. Then I realized the crowd was probably the pool of potential jurors rather than interested spectators. In any case, there was nothing to do but join them, which was bad news; it's difficult enough to take notes on a laptop when you're sitting down and nearly impossible when you're standing up. Not only that, but listening to voir dire examinations of potential jurors is usually boring and tedious even if you're comfortably seated. I'd planned to listen only long enough to get some sense of what the jury pool was like.

So I squeezed between two guys into a spot against the wall. Both men were taller than I was and both had long, unkempt beards. They also were similarly dressed, with striped work shirts and well-worn

dark, stained trousers held up by wide suspenders bearing the logos
of favorite chainsaws. Both also wore heavy boots. Must be loggers.
As I looked around the room, I realized many other men were wearing the same basic uniform, except quite a few also wore dirty, sweat-
stained baseball hats. The atmosphere was redolent with the mixed
odors of wet wool, dirt, male sweat and motor oil, plus a faint but
unmistakable whiff of marijuana. Not all these guys were loggers, I
realized; some undoubtedly were pot farmers, old hippies who had
taken to the woods to grow marijuana before it was legalized in Oregon and were still growing it.

The great majority of the jurors were men, which made me wonder
if women were allowed to vote in this county. But there were a few
women, most of them older, overweight, and dressed in overalls or
thrift-store hand-me-downs. At least they didn't have beards.

I saw one I recognized—Jenny, the waitress who'd served my dinner at the Riverside Café. She was wearing a dress, maybe the only
woman in the room who was.

As I looked around I sensed something missing from the crowd
and finally realized what it was. Unlike virtually every other gathering of people I'd seen in recent years, especially in New York,
nobody had his or her eyes glued to the miniature screen of some
kind of mobile phone or other digital "device." Evidently that
questionable benefit of modern civilization had also yet to reach
Wetside.

Up in the front of the courtroom where I could barely see him,
a guy in what looked like a sheriff's uniform pounded a gavel on a
desk, said hear-ye a couple of times, and everybody who was sitting
down stood up. A door opened behind the bench and a man in a black
robe stepped out. The deputy announced we were in the presence of
the Honorable Judge Emmett Frost.

Frost moved in stately fashion to the bench and sat down behind
it. He was African American, tall and lean, with a narrow fringe of
white hair around his bald, brown pate. I'd read his biography on the

Internet, so I knew he was a former Marine, and he still looked the part. He said something I couldn't hear because all the people who had seats were sitting down in them again. When the noise of all those settling loins had passed, a woman clerk stood up and called the case, "Fremont County Case number CA2306, Cutter versus Steele," and sat down again.

The judge wished everyone a good morning, then launched into the standard boilerplate speech of welcome and gratitude to all the potential jurors for performing their sacred duty as citizens. Looking about the room, I thought a good many of them were probably less concerned with their sacred duty than collecting $20-a-day juror's pay. They looked like they could use the money, though, and I suspected that was what had brought most of them out of their camps and cabins in the woods.

"This is a civil case involving a lawsuit," the judge said. "Nobody is charged with a crime here. The plaintiff, Mr. Mickey Cutter, is author of a book. The defendant, Mr. Clint Steele, also is author of a book. Mr. Cutter's suit accuses Mr. Steele of using some of the material in Mr. Cutter's book in his own book, and Mr. Cutter seeks damages for financial loss plus punitive damages to punish Mr. Steele for his unauthorized use of Cutter's material. That's it in a nutshell. The attorneys in the case are now going to ask you all some questions to determine your qualifications to serve as jurors, but first I need to ask a couple. How many of you are personally acquainted with Mr. Mickey Cutter, the plaintiff in this case?" He pointed to someone up front I couldn't see. "If you are, raise your hand."

Heads swiveled all around the courtroom and nearly half the people raised their hands, including the guys on either side of me. "OK," the judge said. "If you raised your hand, my next question is whether you are prepared to hear this case with an open mind, relying only on the facts you will hear presented, and without favor or prejudice toward Mr. Cutter. If you're unwilling to do that or doubt that you can, please raise your hands again."

Maybe half the people who first raised their hands raised them again. "OK, you're excused," Judge Frost said. "You can leave right now if you like. And thank you again for fulfilling your patriotic duty."

People started getting to their feet. Then one guy in the back shouted, "Do we still get paid?" Many heads turned to hear the answer.

"Don't worry," Judge Frost said. "You get paid just for showing up. The check will be in the mail."

That promise triggered a period of noise as many of the court-room benches—which looked as if they might have been old church pews—were vacated. Those of us left standing against the walls quickly moved in to claim the warm, vacant seats.

What a relief. Thank you, Judge Frost.

The judge continued by asking how many in the jury pool were personally acquainted with the defendant, Clint Steele. He gestured to a man on the right side of the courtroom and I recognized him as the guy with the mouse at the motel, the same one who sold auto-graphed photos of himself on the Internet.

No hands went up.

The judge then went through a list of witnesses and determined that none of them were known to the potential jurors, either. "All right," the judge said. "Now I'd like to introduce the attorneys who will question you about your qualifications to serve as jurors. On my right is Ms. Olivia Pine, who will represent the plaintiff, Mr. Cutter."

I hadn't been able to see her until she stood up. She looked like her name—tall, slim and straight. She had a narrow, serious face with prominent cheekbones, thin lips, a straight nose, and strange, almost transparent eyes. Her hair was out of character with the rest of her; it looked as if someone had dumped a bowl of rotini pasta over her head. Tight, spiral-shaped, pasta-colored curls cascaded in all direc-tions. The pasta color made her look older than she probably was, but it appeared to be her natural color. The curls were natural, too; no permanent could have kept them wound so tightly. She was wearing a

gray pantsuit, peach-colored blouse, and plain black pumps, with no
jewelry, but even in such a simple outfit she was far more splendidly
arrayed than any other woman in the courtroom.

"On my left," Judge Frost said, "is Mr. Merritt Bryce and his associate, Eric Gruen, who will represent the defendant, Mr. Steele."

Bryce and Gruen both stood. The former was obviously the older
of the two. He was a heavyset guy with a rectangular face, a mous-
tache reminiscent of Teddy Roosevelt's, thick, dark, curly hair and
eyebrows, and he wore glasses that made his eyes look about twice
actual size. His associate was a younger copy of him, minus the
glasses. Both men wore expensive dark blue pinstriped suits and regi-
mental ties, and I could see many members of the jury pool looking at
them contemptuously. If they hadn't brought any less formal clothes
with them, I figured Mr. Bryce and Mr. Gruen would be in for a tough
time in this crowd.

Clint Steele was seated next to them. He was wearing black cargo
pants and a powder-blue fishing shirt with his leaping-trout logo on
the pocket. He still had the same neat little black bun of hair in back,
and I noticed some of the jury pool members looking contemptuously at that, too.

"The clerk will now start calling names," Judge Frost said. "If
your name is called, please come forward and take a seat in the
jury box. The attorneys will question each of you individually.
They need to do this to establish your qualifications to hear the
case. There are no necessarily right or wrong answers, so just
relax and tell the truth."

When the box was full of nervous potential jurors, Olivia Pine
stepped forward and addressed the first whose name had been called.
He had a scraggly beard and was dressed like many other men in
the room—striped work shirt, dark work pants and heavy boots. But
unlike most of the others, he was fat, causing the stripes on his shirt
to make major detours on their way down to his belt, which wasn't
visible under the overhang of his belly.

Pine glanced at her notes, then looked up. "Mr. Glenn," she said, "do you know what the word plagiarism means?" Her voice was high and sharp and carried well in the vast wooden acoustics of the old courtroom; if she was as thin as an axe handle, then her voice was the blade, and with her nearly translucent eyes she looked like a force to be reckoned with.

Mr. Glenn frowned and considered. "I'm not sure, but I think it's some kind of a skin disease," he said finally.

Olivia Pine didn't bat an eye. She just asked a couple more questions, then moved on to the next juror. When she reached juror No. 4, she asked the plagiarism question again. This juror, an elderly guy with only three fingers on one hand—obviously a former logger—wrinkled his lean face in concentration, then cleared his throat and said, "I think it's a form of Communism."

That pretty much set the course for the examination of all the jurors. Bryce and Gruen had no better luck when it was their turn, and when I left the courtroom before the lunch recess so I could be assured of a good table at the Riverside, my laptop was empty of notes and it looked as if the attorneys were far from choosing a jury. This jury pool was a blank slate in more ways than one.

I grabbed a turkey sandwich at the café, deciding afterward I didn't feel like returning to the clueless jurors right away, so I headed back to the motel and took a refreshing nap. There were no mice in my room.

I woke up around 2:30 and headed back to the courthouse. I got there just in time to hear the jury impaneled, which was a pleasant surprise; the attorneys must have made great progress in my absence. Nine men and three women were seated in the jury box and one of the women was Jenny, my waitress. Good for her. I also recognized one of the men from the morning's questioning; I couldn't remember his name but recalled he'd said he was a retired forest ranger. He was dressed neatly in a dark green chamois shirt and khaki pants, his hair was combed, and he looked like he had himself together more than anyone else in the jury pool.

Except for those two, the jury was a representative sample of what had been there in the morning. One beefy woman was wearing a sweatshirt and overalls. The sweatshirt had a printed slogan that said, "Bulls Don't," but the rest of it was hidden below the bib of her overalls, so I could only guess at what bulls don't. She also wore what appeared to be a perpetual frown under a fringe of pure white hair surrounding her head like the corona of a solar eclipse. The other woman had a large, round face, dirty glasses and gray hair, and was wearing a big flowery dress that looked as if it had been recycled through the thrift store so many times the flowers had faded to the color of dust.

The eight men besides the forest ranger could have been from a gallery of "wanted" bulletins at the local post office. Five had beards, the others all needed a shave. They wore a variety of stained work shirts, dirty pants, and heavy boots. I remembered one from the morning session; he'd said his occupation was "choke setter," which I figured had something to do with logging, but I wasn't sure what.

Judge Frost, still on the bench, was administering the oath to the jury. When he finished, he said "The lawyers and I have some legal business to attend to, so you are all excused until tomorrow morning when the trial will start at 9 a.m. sharp. We're adjourned until then. Have a good evening."

The jurors filed out and headed for the door, followed by Mickey Cutter and Clint Steele, who didn't speak to one another. That gave me the first chance I'd had for a close-up look at Cutter. Since he was a former basketball coach, I'd expected him to be tall, but he wasn't; I guessed he was about five-feet-ten, with a compact, sinewy build, a well-tanned, friendly face, sharp blue eyes and a well-trimmed wreath of white hair. Olivia Pine, his attorney, was taller than he was. So was Clint Steele.

At 9 a.m. Tuesday the jury was seated in the courtroom, the clerk, bailiff, and court reporter were at their stations, the plaintiff and defendant and their attorneys were where they were supposed to be, and I
was in the second row with my trusty laptop ready to go. Judge Frost
made his appearance, wished everyone an obligatory good morning,
and told the jury the trial would begin with arguments by the attorneys for each side, Olivia Pine first. He also cautioned the jurors that
the arguments did not constitute either testimony or evidence—they
were meant to describe the case each side intended to present—and
when it came time for the jury to decide on a verdict it was to rely
only upon the testimony and evidence. With that, he turned to Olivia
Pine and said, "You're up, Ms. Pine."

She stood to her impressive height and walked gracefully to a point
just in front of the jury box where she stopped and looked each juror
in the eye, one by one. She was wearing a dark blue pantsuit and
cream-colored blouse, again without jewelry, but she still appeared
in a whole different league from any other woman in the courtroom.
Her riotous, pasta-colored hair stuck out in all directions; each curl
wound so tight it looked as if it must hurt.

"Good morning ladies and gentlemen," she began, pacing slowly
back and forth like a sentry in front of the jury box. "My name is
Olivia Pine, and it's my privilege to represent Mr. Mickey Cutter, the
plaintiff in this case, seated over there. He's the person who filed a
lawsuit against the defendant, Mr. Steele, who is over there, next to
his attorneys.

"It's important for you to understand that this is a civil trial, not a
criminal case. Mr. Steele is not accused of a crime. However, we do
believe he did something that caused financial harm to Mr. Cutter,
and Mr. Cutter filed his lawsuit to seek compensation.

"What we allege is that Mr. Steele committed plagiarism. During
the voir dire examination, it appeared some of you were a bit confused
about the meaning of that word, so maybe it would help to start with an
explanation. Plagiarism means the unauthorized use—or theft, if you

will—of another person's words. You may have witnessed plagiarism when you were in school, where it's not uncommon for one student to copy the work of another and submit it as his or her own. That type of plagiarism usually doesn't harm anyone, unless the guilty student happens to get caught. But there are circumstances where plagiarism *can* cause harm, including financial loss.

"You may ask how that could be. How can words have monetary value? Isn't the English language, with all its versatility and flexibility, a marvelous gift we all share in common? Don't we all have the right to use the same words, to pluck them automatically from our memories and employ them to communicate with our fellow humans, just as I am doing now with you? Isn't the language, with its infinite capacity to express love or hate, anger or happiness, or virtually anything in human experience, available for the free use of any of us? The answer is, yes, most of the time—but not always. Sometimes words become property, and you trespass upon them at your own risk.

"Let me explain. Let's assume an author has written a highly suspenseful mystery thriller that makes all the bestseller lists. The book is so popular the publisher can't keep up with orders. It sells hundreds of thousands of copies and makes millions of dollars for the publisher and author. Sale of the movie rights means more millions. One of the things that makes the book so popular, probably the most important thing, is its highly dramatic surprise ending. So imagine what happens when another writer steals the ending and publishes it under his or her own name. It's like puncturing a balloon; the value of the original book suddenly plunges to zero, because now the mystery's solution is out there for everyone to see; it's no longer a surprise. That means nobody wants to buy the book anymore, or see the movie, and the millions of dollars flowing to the publisher and author dry up overnight.

"That's an example of how words can have value, sometimes enormous value. But we're not talking about enormous value in this case. Mickey Cutter, the plaintiff, is a retired teacher living on a pension and Social Security. He's a prominent figure in this community, having taught many years at Wetside High School and coached its basketball team. He's also well known locally for his skills as an expert fly fisherman on the Biscuit River, right over there across the street, and you will hear evidence that four years ago he wrote a book titled *Fly Fishing the Biscuit.* The book describes his knowledge of the river and its fish in great detail, knowledge he accumulated over a virtual lifetime of fishing the Biscuit. The book wasn't a best seller; it was never intended to be. But the modest royalties Mr. Cutter received from it were a welcome addition to his otherwise fixed income, which is all that he and his wife have to live on.

"You will also hear evidence that a year ago Mr. Steele published a book called *Eight Great Western Steelhead Rivers,* which included a chapter on the Biscuit. Mr. Steele is much better known as a fly fisherman than Mr. Cutter; in fact, Mr. Steele is famous. *Eight Great Western Steelhead Rivers* was his ninth book. He's also starred in numerous videos, appeared on many television fishing shows, and has his own signature line of fishing tackle and clothing. He writes for several fishing magazines and is probably the most famous fly fisherman in the world. So it's not surprising that *Eight Great Western Steelhead Rivers* was published by a much larger publishing house than Mr. Cutter's book, or that it was advertised widely, which Mr. Cutter's wasn't, or that it sold many more copies than *Fly Fishing the Biscuit.* But testimony will show that it also cut into the modest sales of Mr. Cutter's book.

"But what's wrong with that? We live in a competitive economy, right? Well, what's wrong is that the evidence will prove Mr. Steele didn't just use his own words in his book; he used a lot of Mr. Cutter's words, too. Sometimes he paraphrased them, which means he didn't repeat them word for word but occasionally changed them or added a few words of his own. But sometimes he *did* repeat them word for word, duplicating exactly what Mr. Cutter had written in his book four years earlier. That was wrong. That was what the law defines as aggravated or wanton misconduct with reckless disregard for the rights of others—in this case, Mr. Cutter. And since the evidence will indicate Mr. Steele's book hurt the sales of Mr. Cutter's, under the law Mr. Cutter is entitled to recover damages. That's what we hope to prove in this trial, and it will be up to you, the jury, to determine the amount of those damages.

"To assist you in doing that, we will present testimony and evidence showing how much time and effort Mr. Cutter invested in learning about the river and its fish, compared to the almost negligible amount of time Mr. Steele spent researching his chapter on the Biscuit. We will also show the similarities and duplications between Mr. Cutter's book and Mr. Steele's; we'll even put some of them side by side on a screen so you can see them for yourselves. You'll also hear testimony about the contract Mr. Cutter had with his publisher and the royalties or revenues he received from the sale of his book. Mr. Cutter's publisher will testify his book was copyrighted, which means it was registered with the Library of Congress and protected by law, and he will explain how that law protects the book—and Mr. Cutter's words—from unauthorized or unlawful use.

"Before Mr. Steele can be held responsible for committing plagiarism, however, the law requires us to prove that he had access to Mr. Cutter's book. You will hear testimony that Mr. Steele checked out Mr. Cutter's book from his local library, renewed it twice, and had it in his possession for nearly two months, which was more than adequate time for him to copy everything he wanted from it.

"You will be asked to assess two kinds of damages against Mr. Steele. One is *actual* damage, the amount of money Mr. Cutter actually lost in royalties from sales of his own book because of the use of his words in Mr. Steele's book. That amount, as you will see, is quite small, which is not surprising when you consider the modest sales of Mr. Cutter's book. But it is nevertheless important when you consider that he and his wife are living on a relatively small fixed income.

"The other assessment you will be asked to make concerns *punitive* damages. These are meant to penalize Mr. Steele, to teach him a lesson so he does not again act with aggravated or wanton misconduct and reckless disregard for the rights of others; in other words, so he does not commit plagiarism again. The law limits punitive damages in this type of case to $250,000, and that is the amount we are asking you to levy against Mr. Steele. So, when you've heard all the testimony and evidence, we will ask you to assess the maximum of both actual and punitive damages. Thank you."

Every word had been spoken without notes. It was an impressive performance, and when she had finished, Olivia Pine—looking every bit as fresh and composed as when she started—returned to her chair, took a sip of water from a glass on the table, and sat down.

"Mr. Bryce?" the judge said.

Merritt Bryce had come to court wearing another expensive pinstriped suit, which I thought almost certainly meant he hadn't brought anything less formal, but now he stood and carefully removed his jacket, revealing a pair of shocking pink suspenders, but without any chainsaw logos. He hung the jacket over the back of his chair and rolled up the sleeves of his startlingly white shirt, just as if he was one of the boys getting ready to go out and cut down a few trees. Gruen, his sidekick, remained impeccably attired in his own expensive suit. Some of the scruffy, disheveled male members of the jury cast disapproving looks at both attorneys.

Bryce took position about ten feet in front of the jury box, spread his legs, and planted his feet as if he meant to stay there all day. It wasn't warm in the courtroom, but I could already see beads of sweat on his ample brow.

"Ladies and gentlemen, my name is Merritt Bryce, as you may recall," he began. "With me is my associate, Eric Gruen. We are proud to represent Mr. Clint Steele, who is seated with us at the table on my right.

"You have just heard Ms. Pine call Mr. Steele a famous man, and she is correct. He is famous because he has worked hard every day of his life to earn the reputation he now enjoys. If any of you are fly fishers, you've undoubtedly heard his name.

"But as happens so often to celebrities in our society—whether they have achieved their status in sports, the arts, politics, or any other field—Mr. Steele's fame has made him a target. Some people think that because he's well known he must have money, lots of it, and there's always someone out there trying hard to get some of it. The truth is that Mr. Steele is not wealthy, not even close, and what little he has is the result of his own untiring labor.

"But what little he has is also at risk in this trial, because even if you find that he did not plagiarize Mr. Cutter's work—as we are confident you will—there will always be some people who will think otherwise, and that will injure Mr. Steele's reputation and his liveli-hood. People will stop buying his books, watching his videos and TV shows, and buying his products, because all those things depend on the reputation Mr. Steele has worked so long and hard to establish. That means that even if Mr. Steele wins this trial, he loses. Please keep those facts in mind as you evaluate the testimony and evidence you are about to hear.

"Ms. Pine has offered you her definition of plagiarism, but she didn't mention the well-known and long-established legal doctrine known as fair use. As you will hear in testimony, fair use means that a writer's published words, even if protected by copyright, can be used lawfully and published by someone else so long as such use does not detract from the value of the original work. In this case, that means that if you find similarities or duplications between Mr. Cutter's book and Mr. Steele's—and we do not expect you will find very many, if any—then Mr. Steele's use of similar language is protected under the doctrine of fair use, so long as it did not hurt the value of Mr. Cutter's book, which we believe it did not.

"We will also introduce the testimony of an expert who will point out that if there *is* any evidence of similarity between the two books— and we do not believe there is—then it is almost certainly due to coincidence. That's not surprising if you think about it. Despite the glory and flexibility of our language, as Ms. Pine so eloquently described it, there really are just a few words you can use to describe what a river looks like, or sounds like, or feels like. Nor are there more than a few different words you can use to describe what a fish looks like, or how it behaves, or what it feels like to catch one. Just ask yourself how many different words you can think of to describe any of these things. I'm sure you'll find the answer is: not many. So it's hardly surprising if Mr. Cutter and Mr. Steele both used the same words in their books. What would be surprising is if they didn't.

"In this case, the key question you must consider is whether Mr. Steele's chapter on fishing the Biscuit River contains passages that might be construed as similar or even identical to some of the material in Mr. Cutter's book and, if so, whether that similarity, if it exists, actually hurt sales of Mr. Cutter's book. Testimony will show conclusively that if Mr. Steele's book had any adverse impact at all upon sales of Mr. Cutter's book, that impact was so slight as to be almost negligible. In other words, it didn't amount to anything, surely not enough to warrant a finding that Mr. Cutter is entitled to actual damages. And if there are no actual damages, then there cannot be any punitive damages, because Mr. Steele did nothing to deserve punishment. That is what we intend to prove."

"So when this is all over and you've heard all the testimony and evidence, we are confident you will come to the conclusion that Mr. Cutter's complaint is utterly without merit. That is not only the correct conclusion, but also, in this case, the only fair one, because, as you will remember, even if he wins this trial, Mr. Steele stands to suffer at least some damage to his reputation and livelihood. You can minimize that damage by finding that he did nothing wrong. Thank you."

Bryce pivoted and returned to his table, pausing to reach into a pinstriped pocket and withdraw a handkerchief with which he wiped his sweaty forehead.

"OK, that concludes the opening statements," Judge Frost said. "We'll take a short recess before the attorneys begin presenting their testimony and evidence. Ms. Pine will go first, then Mr. Bryce."

After the jurors returned from their pit stop, Judge Frost asked Olivia Pine to call her first witness. She stood and said, "the plaintiff calls Ms. Louise Schlechter."

The bailiff got up and headed for the courtroom doors, where the witnesses were waiting outside. It was the first of many such trips he would make in the next couple of days, but it looked as if he could use the exercise. He returned escorting a slim, gray-haired woman wearing eyeglasses on a beaded chain. The clerk administered the oath, and Ms. Schlechter seated herself in the witness chair. She spelled her name for the benefit of the court reporter (and me), gave her address, and said her occupation was librarian.

Olivia Pine elicited the information that Ms. Schlechter was manager of the computer system her local library used to check out books and videos. As she described it, the system virtually automated the process—library users scanned their cards under a barcode reader, then scanned barcodes on items they wished to check out, so they never had to deal with a real live librarian.

"What is the checkout period for a book?" Pine asked.

"Three weeks, unless the book has been placed on reserve. In that case it's two weeks."

"And how long is that information—when a book was checked out and returned—saved in the library database?"

"Five years. The law requires us to save it."

"Thank you. Ms. Schlechter, did you receive a subpoena from my office asking you to search your records to see if Mr. Clint Steele, the defendant in this proceeding, has a library card?"

"Yes."

"What did you find?"

"Mr. Steele does have a library card."

Pine went to her table, picked up a piece of paper and showed it to the witness. "Ms. Schlechter, can you identify this document?"

"Yes, it's the copy I made of Mr. Steele's library card."

"Your Honor, I would like to have this marked and placed in evidence as Plaintiff's Exhibit No. 1," Pine said.

Judge Frost asked Bryce if he had any objections. He didn't, so the document was marked Plaintiff's Exhibit No. 1 by the clerk and placed in evidence.

Pine resumed her questioning. "Ms. Schlechter, did the subpoena also ask you to search Mr. Steel's records in the computer system to see if he ever checked out a book titled *Fly Fishing the Biscuit,* by Mickey Cutter?"

"Yes. I searched and found Mr. Steele checked out the book two years ago on April 22. That meant it was due May 13, but Mr. Steele renewed it May 12 for another three weeks. That meant it was due June 2, but on June 1 he renewed it another three weeks. The book was finally returned June 22, the day it was due."

Pine retrieved two more documents from her table, which the witness identified as computer printouts showing the dates the book had been checked out, renewed and returned. Both were offered and admitted in evidence as Plaintiff's Exhibits 2 and 3.

"So, if my math is correct," Pine said, turning back to the witness, "these exhibits show Mr. Steele had the book for a total of sixty-one days. Is that right?"

"Yes, that's right."

"Thank you very much, Ms. Schlechter. I have no further questions."

"Now it's Mr. Bryce's turn to question the witness, if he chooses," Judge Frost told the jury. "We call this cross-examination. Mr. Bryce, do you have questions for Ms. Schlechter?"

"Indeed I do," he said, rising from his chair and wiping his brow again. Approaching the witness box, he assumed his customary stance. "Ms. Schlechter," he said, "if I correctly understood your explanation of the library computer system, it's possible for someone to check out a book without ever dealing directly with a librarian. Is that right?"

"Yes. That's the way the system was designed to work."

"And you, personally, never see the person who checks out the book. Is that right?"

"Yes."

"So how can you be certain that the book *Fly Fishing the Biscuit* was actually checked out by Mr. Steele?"

"Well, it was checked out to his library card."

"But neither you nor anyone else at the library ever saw him, did they?"

"Not to my knowledge, no. But there was no reason why we would have seen him."

"Isn't it possible that someone else could have been using his card?"

"I suppose it's remotely possible, but it's highly unlikely. We do have occasions when a wife will use her card to check out a book for her husband, or vice versa, but in those cases the system records the book was checked out to one spouse or the other, so it's not as if we didn't know who had the book."

"But you cannot say, with absolute one-hundred-percent certainty, that the book in question was checked out by Mr. Steele, can you?"

"Since you put it that way, no, I can't."

"You testified the book was renewed twice. How was it renewed?"

"I can't answer that. The system only records the fact of renewal."

"Could it have been done online or by email?"

"Yes. In fact, most renewals are done that way."

"So you can't say with absolute one-hundred-percent certainty that Mr. Steele was the one who renewed the book?"

"Not with absolute one-hundred-percent certainty, no."

"So would it be fair to say, Ms. Schlechter, that you have no positive way of knowing that Mr. Steele was the person who checked out and/or renewed the book?"

"I don't . . . "

"Thank you," Bryce interrupted. "No further questions."

Olivia Pine tried to repair the damage by getting the witness to say there was a less than one percent probability that someone other than Clint Steele had checked out the book, but it sounded to me like this round had gone to Merritt Bryce and his client.

At that point Pine asked for a ten-minute recess to set up a screen and projector. Judge Frost granted the recess. It actually went on more than fifteen minutes, as ten-minute recesses always do, before the judge gaveled court back to order and asked Pine to call her next witness.

"The plaintiff calls Mr. Martin Kohl," she said.

The deputy repeated his go-fetch routine and returned escorting a man who looked like he could take care of himself. He was more than six feet tall with dark hair, dark eyes, and a jaw that preceded the rest of his angular face. He was dressed in blue jeans and a yellow canvas shirt. After taking the oath, he took his seat, spelled his name for the court reporter and me, and stated his occupation as crew supervisor at the county road shop.

"Mr. Kohl, are you acquainted with Mickey Cutter, the plaintiff in this case?" was Pine's first question.

"Yes. He's one of my closest friends."

"How do you happen to know Mr. Cutter?"

"He was my history teacher at Wetside High and my varsity basketball coach."

"And your acquaintance continued after you graduated from high school?"

"Yes. I met him one day on the river—the Biscuit—when I was trying to learn how to fly fish. He took me under his wing and taught me just about everything I know about the sport. We still fish together all the time."

"So you also knew that Mr. Cutter wrote a book about fishing the Biscuit?"

"Sure. He signed a copy for me. I still have it, though it's pretty well used."

Pine picked up a book from her table, had Kohl identify it as a copy of *Fly Fishing the Biscuit* and, without objection from Merritt Bryce, had it marked and placed in evidence as Plaintiff's Exhibit No. 4. Returning to the witness, she asked Kohl if he had read the book more than once.

"Oh, yes. I've read it many times. I've practically memorized it."

"Can you briefly summarize the book?"

"Sure. It gives a detailed description of almost every pool, run, and riffle in the Biscuit from the Narrows all the way down to tidewater, and tells how to approach and fish each one at different water levels. It also recommends fly patterns and what time of day to use them and describes the timing of summer and winter steelhead runs. Besides that, it has a lot of good fishing stories."

"Thank you. Mr. Kohl, are you acquainted with Clint Steele, the defendant in this case?"

"Only by reputation."

"So you know he has written a number of fishing books?"

"Yes."

"Have you read any of them?

"Yes.

She picked up another book from her table and asked Kohl to identify it.

"It's a copy of Steele's *Eight Great Western Steelhead Rivers*," Kohl said.

"Have you read it?"

"Yes."

Pine repeated the ritual of having the book admitted to evidence, then asked Kohl how he originally heard about the book.

"I saw it advertised in a fly-fishing magazine," he replied

"And you ordered a copy?"

"Yes."

"Why?"

"The ad said it had a chapter about the Biscuit, and I was curious to see what it said."

"So you read that chapter with particular interest?"

"Yes. I wanted to compare it with Mickey's book."

"You mean Mr. Cutter's book, Plaintiff's Exhibit 4?"

"That's right."

"What was your reaction when you read Mr. Steele's chapter about the Biscuit?"

"Well, right away I noticed a lot of similarities."

Bryce was on his feet immediately. "Objection, Your Honor. There's no foundation for this testimony, and Ms. Pine has not established any qualifications for Mr. Kohl to make a statement like that."

The judge looked at Bryce and frowned. "Mr. Bryce, are you insinuating that the witness is not able to read?"

Bryce, whose face reddened suddenly, gulped and said "No, Your Honor. I withdraw the objection."

The judge nodded at Pine to resume.

"Mr. Kohl, what did you do when you noticed all the apparent similarities between the language in Mr. Cutter's book and Mr. Steele's?" she asked.

"I circled them in ink so I could easily find them again in both books."

"How many segments did you end up circling?"

"I didn't count them, but I think there must have been at least three dozen."

"What did you do then?"

"I went to see Mickey—I mean, Mr. Cutter—and showed him what I'd done."

"What was his reaction?"

"Well, he rarely shows much emotion, but I know him well enough that I could see little signs that he was angry. He asked if he could keep the books awhile and study them at greater length, and I agreed."

"What happened next?"

"He returned the books, told me he'd spoken with his publisher and a lawyer and had decided to file suit against Steele."

Pine went to her table, picked up a small object, and handed it to Kohl. "Can you identify this?" she asked.

Kohl examined it. "Yes," he said, "it's the computer thumb drive on which I stored digital images of the segments I marked in both books so they could be shown side by side for comparison purposes." Pine asked to have the box and its contents marked and placed in evidence as Plaintiff's Exhibit 6.

Judge Frost looked at Bryce, who drew himself up to full height. "Your Honor, for the record, I would like to renew the objection I made when we discussed this in chambers."

"Your objection is noted and overruled again," the judge said. "The exhibit will be admitted in evidence. Ms. Pine, please continue."

Whatever had been discussed earlier in chambers, it sounded as if Pine had prevailed.

"Your Honor, I would like the court's permission to show the images in Plaintiff's Exhibit 6," she said.

"Granted," the judge said.

Pine went to the projector table, turned on the projector, opened her laptop, and inserted the thumb drive. The screen was positioned where I couldn't see it from my seat on the left side of the courtroom, so I transferred immediately to a pew on the right. There were only three or four other people in the courtroom, all "regular" court watchers who had come in to get out of the rain, so finding a seat was no problem.

Pine nodded to the bailiff, who retreated to a series of wall-mounted switches and turned off the overhead lights. Light still came through the windows on both sides, but since it was a dark, rainy day outside, the courtroom darkened noticeably.

When all was ready, Pine turned to address the jury. "Ladies and gentlemen, what you're about to see is a comparison of the segments Mr. Kohl marked in Mr. Cutter's and Mr. Steele's books," she said. "Please read them carefully and see if you agree with Mr. Kohl that there are many similarities."

A pair of slides appeared side by side on the screen:

Cutter Foreword (page i)	Steele (page 204)
The Biscuit is a rain-fed river, rising in coastal mountains where rain is abundant and frequent. Its headwaters are a series of small creeks that flow from the high country in shadowed canyons, creeks with names like Blaze, Spar, Harvey's, Bitter, Spruce and Fog, and finally join one another to form a juvenile river that soon grows larger with the addition of other tributaries as it makes its way first south, then abruptly turns west to begin a sixty-mile flow to the sea.	The Biscuit is a rain-fed river, rising in coastal mountains where rain is abundant and frequent. Its headwaters are a series of small creeks that flow from the high country and finally join to form an infant river that soon grows more robust with the addition of other tributaries as it makes its way first south, then abruptly turns west to begin a sixty-mile journey to the sea.

Pine waited a few moments for the jurors to read the two paragraphs. A few appeared to read quickly while several others moved their lips as they read. The judge waited patiently for them to finish, then told Pine to move on.

She put up two more slides. "What are we looking at here, Mr. Kohl?"

"The slide on the left is from page ii of Mickey Cutter's foreword. The one on the right is from page 205 of Mr. Steele's book."

Cutter Foreword (page ii)	Steele (page 205)
There are two runs of steelhead in the Biscuit. The summer steelhead come first, usually about the time June becomes July. They trickle in steadily until late September, and although there never seem to be a great many of them, they spread quickly throughout the river and if you know where and how to look you can usually find them somewhere.	The summer steelhead come first, usually about July 1. They trickle in steadily until late September, and though there never seem to be a great many of them, they spread quickly throughout the river, so if you know where to look you can usually find them somewhere.
The winter run is much larger and usually bursts into the river during the first big freshet of December. This vanguard is followed by a steady stream of latecomers, and they all join together and rest in the lower pools until mid-February, when the business of spawning begins. So during those seasons—July through September and December into February—the Biscuit offers fly-fishing opportunities worthy of pursuing.	The winter run is much larger and usually arrives in December. The vanguard is followed by a steady stream of latecomers, and they join together to rest in the lower pools until the middle of February, when spawning begins. During those months, from July through September and December into February, the Biscuit offers superlative fly-fishing opportunities.

More slides followed until Judge Frost called a recess for lunch. I headed to the Riverside, followed by the bailiff, who escorted the jury to the restaurant. They sat at a table in a corner and ate without much conversation. I had a "Biscuit Burger," a thick slab of overcooked meat, onions, tomatoes, mysterious sauce, and overcooked French fries.

Court resumed at 1:30 p.m., and Kohl's slide show continued with a comparison of what Cutter and Steele had written about part of the Biscuit called the Whiskey Creek Run.

Cutter (page 67)	Steele (page 271)
The Whiskey Creek Run is accessible by a short walk from the end of Forest Service Road 6248. The creek issues full-blown from a rocky cleft back in the woods on the north side of the Biscuit and runs about a hundred yards to the river where its forceful current joins the main flow, and together they have carved a deep slot against the Biscuit's north bank.	From River Road turn off on Forest Service Road 6248 and follow it to the end. Then it's just a short walk to the Whiskey Creek Run, one of the most dependable steelhead holes on the Biscuit. The creek issues from a spring back in the woods and flows about a hundred yards to the river. There it joins the main current and together they have hollowed out a deep slot against the north bank.
That slot is one of the most dependable steelhead holes on the Biscuit, especially if you're the first angler to fish it in the morning before sunlight falls on the river.	To reach the slot you have to wade out at least sixty feet upstream. The water here is deep and fast, so be careful. When you're in position, start casting a sinking line and wet fly diagonally toward the bank and work your way down.

To reach it you must wade carefully through deep, fast water to a spot at least 60 feet above the slot, then start casting diagonally back toward the bank and work your way down. Use a wet fly.

The slot fishes best in August, when the river is low and the water warming. Steelhead gang up in the slot then to bask in the colder water from the creek, or so the theory goes.

But there's another theory: Back in the days of Prohibition, an old Tarheel named McGregor used water from the creek to make moonshine whiskey, and tradition has it that his still leaked so badly that some of the moonshine got into the creek and steelhead lined up in the slot in hopes of savoring a drop or two. I don't know if that's true, but one memorable day I hooked four steelhead in the slot and I can testify that none of them had a hangover.

During late summer warm water steelhead seek out the slot because they like the cold water of the creek. Best fishing is in the morning before the sun hits the water.

Local legend has it that during Prohibition an old Scotsman used water from the creek to make moonshine whiskey. His still reportedly leaked and some of the booze got into the creek, and locals swear the steelhead lined up in the slot in hopes of having a wee dram. My advice, however, is to bring your own.

After a few more comparisons, the slide show ended and the bailiff restored the lights. Pine then asked Kohl to identify paper enlargements of the images on the thumb drive and asked the judge to enter them in evidence. Bryce again objected, was overruled, and the enlargements became Plaintiff's Exhibit 7. Then Pine thanked Kohl and said she had no further questions.

Bryce took the floor. "Mr. Kohl," he asked, "do you have a college education?"

"Yes. I have an associate degree in construction management."

"Construction management. Did your curriculum include any courses in English?"

"Not that I remember."

Bryce paused to wipe his brow, which seemed to sprout perspiration every time he stood up. "Are you a writer, Mr. Kohl?" he asked.

"No."

"Is there anything in your educational or professional experience that equips you to judge the work of writers?"

"Well . . . I suppose only my personal taste."

"You read a lot of books?"

"I don't have time to read very many."

"Yes, I can see you're a busy man. But my point is, you don't have the training or expertise to compare Mr. Cutter's work with Mr. Steele's or with anyone else's, do you?"

Kohl's eyes narrowed and a pair of lines on his forehead deepened. "I guess that's your opinion, Mr. Bryce."

"Yes it is." He spent another half hour grilling Kohl about what words he would have used to describe the Biscuit, its waters, fish, and fly patterns without repeating the same words Cutter used. In most cases Kohl was unable to think of very many, if any. It was a pretty effective cross-examination.

Olivia Pine had no questions on redirect, and Judge Frost declared another ten-minute recess that went on for fifteen minutes before court resumed and Pine called her next witness, Gregory Bosenko. I was surprised when the bailiff returned with the pudgy guy who checked me in at the Spruce Grove Motel. He was sworn, took his seat, spelled his name for the court reporter and me, and gave his occupation as owner and proprietor of the Spruce Grove Motel.

"Mr. Bosenko, how long have you owned the Spruce Grove Motel?" Pine asked.

"Twelve years."

"And do you keep records of all your guests?"

"Yeah, of course."

"Do you keep them on a computer?"

"Yeah, sure."

"Mr. Bosenko, are you acquainted with Clint Steele, the defendant in this case?"

"That's him sitting over there. He's staying at my motel now."

"Is this the first time he's stayed there?"

"No. He stayed with me two years ago."

"How do you happen to know that?"

"You asked me to check my records, and that's what I found."

"How long did he stay on that occasion?"

"Two nights."

"Just two nights?"

"Yeah," he said, glaring at Steele. "I'd forgotten about that until you asked me to look. That's when I remembered; he complained about finding a mouse in his room and I had to give him a room on the house. He pulled the same stunt last night and I gave him another free room, the miserable, rotten cheat."

Bryce jumped to his feet. "Your Honor! Move to strike! Irrelevant and prejudicial!"

Judge Frost quietly instructed the court reporter to delete Bosenko's last words and ordered the jury to disregard them. He also told Bosenko to keep his opinions to himself. Bosenko merely nodded, as if he weren't sorry at all for what he'd said.

Pine retrieved a document from her apparently inexhaustible collection, offered it to Bosenko and asked if he could identify it.

"Yeah," he said. "It's a computer printout of Steele's registration when he stayed at the motel two years ago." Pine offered it in evidence, Bryce did not object, and the document became Plaintiff's Exhibit 8.

Pine zeroed in again. "Mr. Bosenko, when Mr. Steele stayed with you two years ago, do you recall the purpose of his visit?"

"Yeah. I think he said he was doing research for a book."

"A book about the Biscuit River?"

"Yeah, I think that was it."

"But he stayed only two days?"

"That's right."

"Thank you. No further questions."

Bryce was quick to cross-examine. "Mr. Bosenko, the Spruce Grove is the only place in town where people can stay, is that right?"

"Yeah."

"There are no other motels or beds-and-breakfasts or anything like that?"

"No."

"But there are three Forest Service campgrounds nearby, are there not?"

"Uh, yeah, I guess that's right."

"And you don't know whether Mr. Steele might have camped at one or more of them, do you?"

"No, I can't say I do."

"Did you know people are allowed to stay up to fourteen days in those campsites?"

"No, I didn't know that."

"So you didn't know that if he stayed in all three he could have stayed forty-two days? Or even longer if he went back to one or more of them after his first two-week stay?"

"No, I didn't know that, either."

"So Mr. Steele could have spent six weeks or even longer in those campgrounds and you never would have known it, is that right?"

"I suppose so."

"I suppose so, too. No further questions."

Pine had no redirect and by then it was close to 5 o'clock, so Judge Frost adjourned until 9 o'clock the next morning.

I tried the Riverside's chicken-fried steak for dinner. It wasn't bad, but I wouldn't recommend the gravy. After that I returned to my room and spent some time on my laptop, cleaning up the day's notes. Then I turned on the TV and began searching for intelligent life, but found none, as usual, so I stretched out in the swale on my bed and resumed reading the paperback I'd started on the plane to Portland.

I hadn't been reading long when I heard a cautious tap on my door. Wondering who it could be, I got up, went to the door and looked out through the peephole. The peephole lens distorted the face on the other side but my brain finally assimilated the pieces and I recognized the face belonged to Eric Gruen, Merritt Bryce's young associate. What the hell could he want? I unhooked the safety chain and opened the door.

"Mr. Kane," he began, but I interrupted to ask how he knew my name. He looked surprised. "Uh, everybody knows who you are and why you're here," he said.

That was great news. I thought I'd been maintaining anonymity, which is how I like it. I supposed Bosenko had learned who I was when Gladys made my reservation and spread the word around. "Well, what can I do for you?"

"I'm sorry to disturb you, but I really need to talk to you. It's very important."

"I suppose you'd better come in then." I held the door open and gestured to one of the beat-up chairs at the beat-up table. He took it, and I took the other.

Gruen seemed nervous. He squirmed in the chair, which made dangerous noises, then finally said, "I'm here at the request of our client, Mr. Steele."

I waited for him to continue.

He cleared his throat. "Uh, as you heard Mr. Bryce say in his opening argument, Mr. Steele is very concerned about what this trial could do to his reputation. He's afraid it will suffer no matter how the trial turns out. His whole livelihood rests on his reputation and, as Mr. Bryce said, even if we win, Mr. Steele could lose."

He paused, evidently waiting for me to say something. I didn't. "So, anyway," he continued, "Mr. Steele has asked me to make you an offer." He cleared his throat again. "Mr. Steele is prepared to write you a check for ten thousand dollars in exchange for your written agreement not to write anything about this trial, no matter how it turns out."

It took a moment for that to register. Then I asked why Steele hadn't come to see me himself.

"I'm not sure," Gruen said. "Maybe he was embarrassed. I don't know."

"If I were him, I'd be embarrassed, too. Do you realize what he's asking? He wants me to risk my reputation and my livelihood in order to save his."

"Uh, I hadn't thought of it that way."

"Well, that's how I think of it. Why don't you just offer Mickey Cutter a settlement? Then there'd be no trial and no story."

"We tried that, but Mr. Cutter refused." Gruen winced, probably realizing too late that he shouldn't have volunteered that information.

"Well, now that you've done your duty, you can tell Steele I refused, too."

"I was afraid you'd say that." He placed his hands on the table, which also made dangerous noises, and pushed himself out of the chair. "Sorry I bothered you." He started for the door, then paused and turned to face me again. "Mr. Steele told me that if you refused his offer, he's prepared to go up to twenty thousand dollars."

"You can tell Mr. Steele the answer is still no and it will always be no, I don't care how high he's willing to go."

"I'll tell him that. Good evening to you, Mr. Kane." He opened the door and stepped outside. The porch light was on and I could see beyond the overhang that it was still raining.

When the trial resumed next morning Olivia Pine called Mickey Cutter as her first witness. After eliciting routine information about his education and background, she finally got to the point: "Mr. Cutter, how many years have you been fishing the Biscuit River?"

"Since I was five or six years old. That's when my father started taking me."

"And how old are you now?"

"Seventy-two."

"So you've been fishing the river more than sixty years. Have you always been a fly fisherman?"

"Well, that's how my father got me started, but it was a few years before I really learned how to cast. Or wade."

"So your father spent many years fishing the Biscuit, too?"

"Yes. In fact, he named some of the pools on the river."

"And he taught you those names?"

"Yes. After he was gone I added a few of my own."

"You mean that you named some of the river's pools?"

"Yes, some that didn't have names before. I suppose it was presumptuous of me, but the names seem to have stuck."

"And those are now the names listed in your book?"

"That's right."

"How old were you when you caught your first steelhead, Mr. Cutter?"

"I was eleven years old then, but I still remember it as if it happened yesterday."

"Tell us about it."

"It was in the pool we call the Deep Throat. I was fishing a Green-butt Skunk on a sinking line when I had the hardest strike I'd ever experienced and suddenly this big, bright, gleaming fish threw itself into the air and started running like crazy. I was so excited I thought my heart might burst right out of my chest, and for a moment I just stood there and let the fish have its way. It ran to the end of the pool and took all my line and most of my backing before I woke up and started trying to follow it. It jumped four more times—I still remember counting each jump—and made a couple more long runs and I guess it must have been fifteen or twenty minutes before it tired enough for me to lead it to the beach. It was a bright female summer-run fish, about seven-and-a-half pounds, and I removed the hook—it was barbless—and returned it to the river, as my father taught me."

"Tell us about some of your other experiences on the river."

Merritt Bryce stood up. "Objection, Your Honor," he said. "This is all very interesting, but I fail to see the relevance."

"Ms. Pine?" Judge Frost queried.

"The relevance will soon become apparent, Your Honor."

"Very well. See that it does. Objection overruled."

Steele's head swiveled back and forth as he followed the colloquy between the attorneys and the judge, making the neat little bun of hair on the back of his head bob back and forth like a black tennis ball.

Pine resumed questioning. "Mr. Cutter, you were about to tell us some of your other noteworthy experiences."

"Yes. Well, I was fifteen when I caught my first steelhead on a dry fly in the Biscuit. It was the fourteenth of July, early in the morning, and I was fishing a place we call Anna's Glide; it's still maybe the finest piece of dry-fly water on the river. I was using a floating line and fishing downstream with a riffle-hitched fly called the Purple Peril. The fly was tied at an angle to the leader so it would skid across the surface, throwing up a little wake behind it. The fish can really see that from below and sometimes they'll rise to take it, and that's what happened that morning. I saw this great fish suddenly burst out of the water and seize the fly and it hooked itself and started running downstream. I'd never seen anything like that before in my life, and I damn near wet my pants. Oops! Sorry, Your Honor. Anyway, I got the fish, a beautiful, bright buck summer steelhead of about nine pounds."

"What's the largest steelhead you've ever taken in the Biscuit?"

"That was in the winter, the day after my sixtieth birthday. I thought it was a belated gift. I was fishing the Bunkhouse Pool with a fly we call the Rusty Rabbit when I felt a sudden long, slow, powerful pull. The fish fought deep and was hard to move, so I knew it was big, and we traded line for—I don't know—maybe fifteen minutes before I got my first look at it. When I finally got it to the beach I could see it was a buck with a bright red stripe down its side, and I knew it was the largest fish I'd ever landed. It measured thirty-seven inches and on my pocket scale it weighed seventeen-and-a-half pounds. That's an unusually big fish for the Biscuit."

"Mr. Cutter, how is it you remember these things so well?"

"Well, they just seem to engrave themselves in my memory. But it also helps a lot that I keep a journal."

"A journal of all your fishing experiences?"

"Yes, that's right."

"And did you rely upon your journal when you wrote your book about fly fishing the Biscuit?"

"Oh, yes. It was indispensable for that purpose."

"So you had written records of . . . what, more than sixty years of fishing experience on the river?"

"Well, more than fifty years anyway. I didn't start keeping the journal until I caught that first steelhead when I was eleven."

"Why did you write your book, Mr. Cutter?"

"Well, I'd acquired all that knowledge and experience and I figured it would be selfish to keep it to myself. And I'm not getting any younger, as you can see, so I thought it would be a good idea if

I could share some of that knowledge with other fly fishers. Like my friend Martin Kohl."

"Do you know of anyone else with as much experience on the river?"

Cutter thought for a moment, then said he did not.

"All right," Pine said, "then let me ask this: Mr. Cutter, you mentioned your friend Martin Kohl. You heard his testimony here yesterday, right?"

"Yes."

"And he was the one who first showed you a copy of Mr. Steele's book, is that right?"

"Yes."

"And you heard and saw his testimony about the similarities between your book and Mr. Steele's?"

"Yes."

"In your opinion, was Mr. Kohl's testimony complete and accurate?"

"Yes, except for one important thing."

"And what was that?"

"His testimony about the Whiskey Creek Run didn't mention what happened to it."

"What did happen to it?"

"Two years after my book was published we had an unusually severe winter flood on the Biscuit. It caused the riverbank above the Whiskey Creek Run to collapse and the rubble completely filled the deep slot against the north bank. There hasn't been a steelhead in that spot since and it's no longer fishable."

"What's the significance of that?"

"Well, it means the Whiskey Creek Run was gone even before Mr. Steele came here to do research for his book, so the only way he could have gotten the description of the Whiskey Creek Run in his book was by copying the one in mine, which by then was already a year or so out of date."

Bryce popped up again; he was certainly getting his exercise. "Your Honor, I strongly object to use of the word 'copying.' It's not only highly prejudicial but there's no foundation."

"Your turn, Ms. Pine," the judge said.

"Your Honor, I think Mr. Cutter's testimony already laid the foundation. And if it's prejudicial, Mr. Steele has only himself to blame. He made his bed and now he has to lie in it."

"Anything else, Mr. Bryce?" the judge inquired.

"Yes! I renew my objection. There's no adequate foundation and the term used is extremely prejudicial. I move to strike this testimony."

Judge Frost pondered the matter for a moment before coming to a decision. "I'll allow it," he said.

"Thank you, Your Honor," Pine said. "Now, Mr. Cutter, let me be sure I understand your testimony. You're saying that the Whiskey Creek Run was destroyed in a flood two years after your book was published, and that at the time Mr. Steele says he was here—and Mr. Bosenko's records show he was here—Mr. Steele or anyone else could have found that out by fishing the Biscuit. Is that right?"

"Yes. Or they could have found out just by asking any local fisherman."

"But Mr. Steele's book, published two years *after* the Whiskey Creek Run was destroyed, still offers a description of it very similar to the one in your book. Is that correct?"

"Yes."

"Thank you, Mr. Cutter. No further questions."

Bryce got back to his feet, assumed his familiar stance, and began his cross-examination. "Mr. Cutter, it was your friend Martin Kohl who first suggested to you that Clint Steele's book might have similarities with yours, isn't that right?"

"Yes."

"So you never reached that conclusion independently?"

"Well, when I compared the two books I saw that he was correct."

"But it wasn't your original idea, that's my point. Was it also Mr. Kohl who suggested you should file a lawsuit against Mr. Steele?"

"No."

"Did anyone else?"

"No."

"Did you ask your publisher if he thought you should file suit?"

"I called to ask him what he thought, yes."

"And what did he say?"

"He asked for time to consider the matter and said he'd call me back. When he called he said he could see the reasons for my concern, but he didn't think there was anything he, or I, could do about it."

"Why not?"

"He said he thought the amounts of money involved would be too small to make it worth the trouble or expense to file a lawsuit."

"Did anyone else advise you to file a lawsuit?"

"No."

"So why, Mr. Cutter, did you file suit?"

"Well, seeing what Mr. Steele did—copying my stuff—made me very angry."

Bryce addressed the bench. "Your Honor, again I strongly object to use of the word 'copying.' Whether there was any copying by anyone in this case is a matter for the jury to decide. I move to strike."

"Sustained," Judge Foster said. "The jury will disregard Mr. Cutter's answer. And Mr. Cutter, I must caution you to avoid further use of such prejudicial language."

"Understood, Your Honor," Cutter said, although from the look on his face it was apparent the old coach wasn't used to being admonished.

Bryce picked up where he'd left off. "So you filed suit in anger?"

"Yes."

"Money was not your motive?"

"No, and that's the truth. But asking for monetary damages is the only course the law provides, the only means of punishment I have.

"So punishment is what you're really after?"

"I suppose that's true."

"Mr. Cutter, the publicity that will undoubtedly be forthcoming from this case will do great harm to Mr. Steele's reputation and livelihood, regardless of how this trial turns out. Don't you think that's punishment enough?"

This time it was Olivia Pine who got quickly to her feet. "I object, Your Honor," she said. "Hypothetical and calls for a conclusion by the witness. Also I don't see its relevance."

Judge Frost considered. "Sustained," he said finally. "Time to change direction, Counselor."

Bryce nodded, paused to mop his brow, cleared his throat, and resumed questioning. "Mr. Cutter, is this the only lawsuit you've ever filed?"

"Yes, and I hope it's the only one I'll ever have to file."

"Why do you say that?"

"Because I don't like being questioned by people like you."

The jury broke into laughter, along with the few other people in the courtroom.

Bryce's square face turned crimson, and he returned to his table and pretended to consult some notes. Then he went back to face the witness and elicited the fact that *Fly Fishing the Biscuit* was Cutter's only writing endeavor and, no, he did not consider himself an experienced professional writer. "So what qualifies you to judge the work of Mr. Steele, who *is* an experienced professional writer?" Bryce asked.

"I think the only qualification needed is the ability to read," Cutter answered. "Martin's testimony comparing passages from the two books speaks for itself. It doesn't take a genius or a highly experienced professional writer to figure out what happened."

Whatever answer Bryce was expecting, that wasn't it. He held a brief whispered conversation with Eric Gruen, then apparently decided to throw in the towel before things got worse. "That'll be all with this witness," he told the judge.

I noted he hadn't asked anything about the Whiskey Creek run, probably because he knew the answer would be unfavorable to his client. I wondered if the jury would remember that.

Olivia Pine had no questions on redirect, and Mickey Cutter stepped down. Pine called Lars Lofgren as her next witness. The bailiff scurried up the corridor dividing the gallery and returned followed by a short, rotund man with a long white beard and deep-set blue eyes behind round glasses. If he'd been wearing a red stocking cap he would have looked exactly like Santa Claus, but the top of his head was as bald as a light bulb. He wore gray slacks that needed ironing, an old beige sports jacket with threadbare elbows, a white shirt with yellowed collar, and a lavender tie almost as wide as a baby's diaper. It made me wonder if he was color blind. His shoes squeaked as he walked. Even so, he was the grandest male figure in the courtroom, surpassing even Merritt Bryce and Eric Gruen, who had shed their jackets and rolled up their shirt sleeves.

Lofgren was sworn, squeezed himself into the witness chair and identified himself as owner of Pacific Ocean Press, or POP, publisher of Mickey Cutter's book. In response to Pine's questions, he described details of his contract with Cutter, which called for the author to be paid an advance of $1,000, half payable on signing and half on acceptance of the manuscript. "I know that doesn't sound like a very big number, but we're a small, regional publishing house, Mr. Cutter was an untested author, and the book was aimed at a relatively narrow target market, so it was the best we could do," Lofgren said.

The contract specified royalties of 8 percent of the sale price, which was $19.95, or 88 cents for each book sold at a 45 percent discount to bookstores or online vendors, as virtually all were. The initial press run was 2,000 copies, which, if all the books were sold, would result in $1,760 in royalties. The first $1,000 of that went to the publisher to offset the advance, so Cutter would receive only $760 in addition to the advance.

Copies of the book were sent to the Library of Congress along with a copyright application to give the book legal protection from unauthorized use. Review copies of the book were sent to a couple of regional fishing magazines and the Portland *Oregonian* and Eugene *Register-Guard*, which both published favorable reviews. One of Lofgren's staffers also scheduled readings and signings of the book by Cutter at stores in Portland and Eugene, plus a radio interview. Cutter also promoted the book himself through appearances at several fly-fishing clubs and encouraged people who bought the book to post reviews online, as long as they were favorable.

The first press run sold out in little more than two years and a second printing of 1,500 copies was ordered. The book price was increased to $21.95 for the second printing and, under the contract, the royalties increased to 10 percent. Based on experience with similar books, Lofgren said he expected about 1,000 copies of the second printing would sell in the first year, which would mean another $1,207 in royalties for Cutter; after that sales would slowly decline. The second printing started selling briskly but sales took a nosedive almost immediately after publication of Steele's book. After a year, only 509 books had been sold, resulting in royalties of only $614.

That left 991 books still unsold, and if all had eventually sold it would have meant another $1,196 in royalties for Cutter. Altogether, Lofgren said, the appearance of Steele's book probably cost Cutter $1,810 in royalties.

Bryce immediately attacked that figure on cross-examination. "You mean we're here because of a measly $1,810?" he demanded.

"That's how I figure it," Lofgren said.

"That's ridiculous. It's a waste of everybody's time. Did you advise Mr. Cutter to file suit over that miniscule amount?"

"No. He asked my advice, but I told him not to file suit."

"Why?"

"Well, because I thought the expense of a lawsuit would be far greater than the amount he could recover."

"But he went ahead anyway."

"Obviously."

"Mr. Lofgren, if the publication of Clint Steele's book cost Mr. Cutter some royalties—which I doubt—it must also have cost you some profits, is that not correct?"

"Yes it is."

"So why didn't *you* file suit? Or join Mr. Cutter's?"

"Same reason. I thought the expense would be greater than anything I could recover."

"Thank you, Mr. Lofgren. No further questions."

On redirect, Pine asked Lofgren if he thought publication of Steele's book had hurt sales of Cutter's second printing. "I don't know what else could have caused it," he said.

She also tried to get Lofgren to admit that Cutter's suit was justified because even though the amount of lost royalties was small, the jury could still award a whopping amount of punitive damages that would make it all worthwhile, and Lofgren could have had a share in that by joining the suit. Lofgren reluctantly agreed.

After Lofgren stepped down the judge recessed for lunch and since there was an interval between rain showers we all trekked over to the Riverside, the jurors kept together by the huffing-and-puffing bailiff so they couldn't speak or be spoken to by passersby. They all sat together at the same table in the corner, and when I looked over from my seat at the counter, Jenny the juror gave me a discreet wave. I winked back.

My lunch was a grilled tuna sandwich—the tuna probably came from the coast of Vietnam or someplace like that—garnished with stale potato chips. I made it back to the courthouse just ahead of the next shower.

When Judge Frost gaveled the trial back to order, Pine called her next witness, a man named Trevor Dillon. The bailiff returned from the hallway leading a tall, lanky, mostly bald man with a short white beard, wearing a dark sport coat, tan slacks and a blue shirt open at the collar. He was sworn, gave his name and address, and described his occupation as an attorney with the non-profit Institute for the Study of Intellectual Property. In response to Pine's questions, he defined intellectual property as the product of human thought or creativity, usually expressed in writing, music, art, design, computer software, or some other tangible form which, under the law, may be protected by copyrights, patents, trademarks and so forth. Most of the jurors looked at him as if he were speaking a foreign language. He also recited his curriculum vitae, including advanced degrees, authorship of numerous law journal articles, participation in the trials of several intellectual property cases, and experience as an expert witness in dozens of cases involving plagiarism. In response to Pine's request and without objection from Bryce, Judge Frost certified Dillon as an expert witness.

"Mr. Dillon, did my office engage you to apply the benefit of your experience to analyze the facts of this case?" she asked.

"Yes."

"And did you do so?"

"Yes."

"Can you explain to the jury what you did?"

"Certainly. I read Mr. Cutter's book and Mr. Steele's book very carefully, marked certain passages for word-by-word comparison, then mathematically determined the frequency of words or phrases that were duplicated in those sections. Then I compared the order of presentation in each book; that is, whether each presented the same information in the same or identical order."

"Are those standard tests for plagiarism?"

"Yes, they are.

"And did you form any opinions as a result of these tests?"

"Yes, I did."

"Good, but before I ask you what those are, I want to make sure the jury understands you were not in court to hear the earlier testimony of Mr. Martin Kohl, is that right?"

"Yes."

"So when you said you marked certain passages for comparison in Mr. Cutter's and Mr. Steele's books, those were not the same passages that Mr. Kohl used for comparison, is that correct?"

"Well, I don't know what passages he used, so it's possible some were the same."

"But that would just be a coincidence, right?"

"Yes."

"All right. Now please explain the results of your comparisons."

"I chose some passages at random and others I thought superficially appeared similar or alike, then analyzed each passage and determined by actual count how many words or phrases used in Mr. Cutter's book were also repeated in the same context in Mr. Steele's book. The results showed that in the samples I examined, Mr. Steele used or repeated Mr. Cutter's words or phrases 47.2 percent of the time. I believe that is probably an accurate percentage for the entire text of Mr. Steele's book."

"So you're saying Mr. Steele used Mr. Cutter's words and descriptions nearly half the time, is that right?"

"Yes."

"And you said you also analyzed the order of presentation in the two books?"

"Yes."

"What did you find when you did that?"

"Well, Mr. Cutter began his descriptions of the Biscuit River at the Narrows Pool, which he said is the uppermost fishable pool in the river, and proceeded downstream from there, describing each pool in detail as he went. Mr. Steele did exactly the same thing, but I attach no real importance to that; there's really only two ways you can describe a river in an organized fashion, and that's either downstream or upstream, so it had to be one or the other. What may be of greater significance is that Mr. Cutter described forty-seven pools or runs by name and Mr. Steele listed exactly the same number and used exactly the same names."

"But if the names of those pools were well-established and known to every fisherman, you wouldn't expect anything different, would you?"

"Yes, you'd expect that to be the case, but after a very thorough search I was unable to find any Internet source or any publication other than Mr. Cutter's book where those names are actually given, nor any map where the pools are labeled by name. So I believe Mr. Cutter's book was probably the original source of that information."

"And that would indicate Mr. Steele got the information from Mr. Cutter's book?"

"Yes."

"So taking these analyses and comparisons together, did you reach any definitive opinion?"

"Yes. There's absolutely no doubt in my mind that Mr. Steele plagiarized Mr. Cutter's work. In fact, I'd have to say this is one of the most egregious cases of plagiarism I've ever seen."

I wondered how many members of the jury had ever previously heard the word "egregious."

"Thank you Mr. Dillon," Pine said. "I have no more questions."

That was Merritt Bryce's cue. He took his customary stance like a goalie guarding the net and opened fire. "Mr. Dillon, are you familiar with the doctrine of fair use?"

"Yes, of course, but it does not apply here."

"It doesn't? Why not?"

"Well, for one thing, fair use means just that; you can't use more than is fair. And while courts have resisted trying to establish exactly how much *is* fair, I think any court in the land would agree that Mr. Steele's use of more than 47 percent of Mr. Cutter's words is *not* fair."

Bryce retreated to his table, glanced at a document on top, then returned to the witness. "Mr. Dillon," he said, "how many synonyms can you think of for the word 'river'?"

Several jury members looked as if they were having trouble with the word "synonym."

"Well," Dillon said, "there's 'stream,' 'watercourse,' 'creek,' perhaps 'freshet,' and—I don't know, perhaps others I can't think of offhand."

"How many synonyms can you think of for the word 'pool'"?

Pine stood up. "Your Honor, I fail to see the relevance of this."

"I'm having the same trouble, Ms. Pine," the judge said. "Mr. Bryce, can you enlighten us?"

"Certainly, Your Honor. I'm merely trying to show that, for all its flexibility and versatility, the English language has only so many words to describe common objects like rivers and pools, so it's unrealistic to assert that use of those words by different authors amounts to plagiarism."

"What say you, Ms. Pine?" the judge asked.

"Well, I think we could be here all night if Mr. Bryce wants to go through every word in his client's book."

"I think you could be right. Mr. Bryce, I believe you've already effectively made your point. Objection sustained."

For a moment Bryce looked like a little kid being scolded by its mother, but he finally raised his eyes to the bench and said, "In that case, Your Honor, I have only one more question." He faced the witness and asked Dillon if he was being paid for his testimony.

"Actually, no. Testifying in cases like this is a pro bono service offered by the Institute for the Study of Intellectual Property. I am being reimbursed for expenses, but that's all."

Bryce reacted as if he'd been punched in the gut, but again recovered quickly. "But you are still being paid your regular salary by the institute, are you not?"

"Yes, I am."

"So, in effect, you are being paid to testify, isn't that right?"

"Well, I suppose you could say so."

"I do say so. No further questions, Your Honor."

"Any re-cross, Ms. Pine?" the judge inquired.

"No, Your Honor. The plaintiff rests."

"Very well," Judge Frost said. "Mr. Bryce, you may call your first witness."

"The defense calls Mr. Peter Fairburn," Bryce said, and once more the bailiff hustled up the courtroom aisle. This time he returned with a dapper man with slicked-back gray hair who was wearing an elegant dark suit, blue shirt, and conservative striped tie. Apparently Bryce hadn't warned him to dress down for the jury.

Fairburn identified himself as a partner in the San Francisco law firm of Hatton, Barkley and Fairburn, specializing in intellectual property cases. Responding to Bryce's questions, he rattled off a curriculum vitae nearly as voluminous as Trevor Dillon's. Bryce asked Judge Frost to accept Fairburn as an expert witness and, without objection from Olivia Pine, he did so.

Then Bryce got to the point. "Mr. Fairburn, have you read the two books that are at issue in this trial, Mr. Cutter's book, *Fly Fishing the Biscuit*, and Mr. Steele's book, *Eight Great Western Steelhead Rivers*?"

"Yes, I have."

"And you're aware that in his complaint, Mr. Cutter accuses Mr. Steele of plagiarizing his work?"

"Yes."

"Based on your experience in intellectual property law and your history of trying cases involving plagiarism, did you form any opinion in this case?"

"Yes."

"And what was that opinion?"

"I don't think this was a case of plagiarism."

"How did you arrive at that conclusion?"

"Well, I noted there was some similarity in the words used by both authors, but I attribute most of that to limitations of the English language, not any skullduggery on the part of Mr. Steele. For example, there are only so many words in our language to describe rivers, or fish, or fishing flies, or casting, or wading, and so on, so you would expect there to be similarity or duplication in two books about essentially the same subject. That's especially true since the books are about fly fishing, which has its own terminology and jargon."

"Would you say, then, that any similarity between Mr. Cutter's book and Mr. Steele's falls within the doctrine of fair use?"

"Absolutely."

"In other words, Mr. Steele was within his rights to use such material without crediting Mr. Cutter, the plaintiff, as the author?"

"That's right."

"Thank you, Mr. Fairburn. No further questions."

Pine attacked swiftly on cross-examination. "Mr. Fairburn," she asked, "we have heard previous expert testimony that Mr. Steele used Mr. Cutter's words 47.2 percent of the time in his book—in other words, nearly half the time. Would you describe that as 'fair use'?"

"I would question that figure," he said. "In any case, I stand by my conclusion that anything Mr. Steele used from Mr. Cutter's book was legally allowable under the doctrine of fair use."

"What percentage of copied material would it take for you to concede it wasn't fair use?"

"Objection!" Bryce shouted.

"Sustained," Judge Frost said.

"All right, then I have just one more question," Pine said. "Mr. Fairburn, are you being paid for your testimony here today?"

Fairburn looked even more uncomfortable than he had answering the previous questions. "Yes," he said finally.

"How much?"

"Objection!" Bryce shouted again. "Improper and irrelevant!"

Judge Frost sustained the objection and Pine had no further questions. "Call your next witness, Mr. Bryce," the judge instructed.

"Your Honor, the defendant rests," Bryce said.

That was a shock, at least to me. How could Bryce possibly expect to have a chance of winning this case without putting Clint

Steele on the stand? While I was trying to get my head around that, the judge noted it was getting late in the afternoon and excused the jury so he and the attorneys could work on jury instructions. "We'll resume at 9 o'clock tomorrow morning with final arguments," he said.

While the jurors were leaving, I tried to figure out Bryce's strategy for keeping Steele off the stand. Eventually I realized there were a lot of reasons he might not want his client to testify. Whatever Steele had to say probably wouldn't carry as much weight as what Pine might force him to say while she made him squirm under oath in cross-examination—that he really did keep Cutter's book for two months, as Louise Schlechter testified; that he really did spend only two nights at the Spruce Grove during his "research," as Bosenko testified, and he copied Cutter's description of the Whiskey Creek Run and all the other portions of Cutter's book, as Kohl and Dillon testified. Pine might even force him to admit he'd let a mouse loose in his motel room. On the other hand, if Steele didn't testify, Pine wouldn't be able to ask about any of these things, nor would she be permitted to suggest to the jury that it should draw any conclusions from Steele's silence. All things considered, I thought Bryce might have come up with a brilliant game plan by keeping his client off the stand.

While I considered all this, the judge and attorneys remained at their posts until the jury had gone. Then Judge Frost asked if there were any motions.

Bryce stood. "Yes, Your Honor. The defendant moves for a directed verdict that the defendant's liability has not been proven by a preponderance of the evidence."

The judge didn't even look at Olivia Pine for a response. "The motion is denied," he said. "If there are no other motions, we'll retire to chambers to work on the jury instructions."

No other motions were forthcoming, so the judge and attorneys disappeared into chambers, and I headed for the door.

Precisely at 9 o'clock the next morning Judge Frost emerged from his chambers and bade good morning to the attorneys, their clients, and finally to the jurors, several of whom still had dark spots of fresh rain on their clothing. "Ladies and gentlemen, as you may recall, at the beginning of the trial you heard opening arguments. Now it's time for closing arguments. Each side will have a maximum of forty minutes to make their argument. Ms. Pine again will go first as she did at the beginning of the trial, followed by Mr. Bryce. Then Ms. Pine will have an opportunity to deliver a rebuttal argument if she so chooses, but she must split the time between her opening and rebuttal arguments so they may not exceed forty minutes total. Ms. Pine, are you ready?"

"Yes, Your Honor." She was dressed this morning in dark blue slacks and a plain white blouse with a thin gold chain around her long, graceful neck, though her hair remained as furiously untamed as ever. She stood to her stately height, resumed her measured sentry's pace back and forth in front of the jury box, bade the jurors good morning, and launched into her argument.

"Three days ago at the beginning of this trial—has it been only three days? It seems longer, doesn't it?—I told you this is a civil trial, not a criminal matter. Mr. Steele has not been charged with a crime. But make no mistake; he *is* guilty of what the law calls aggravated or wanton misconduct and reckless disregard for the rights of others. He deliberately stole Mr. Cutter's words and used them in his own book for his own benefit. He was paid for the work Mr. Cutter did, and he was paid more than Mr. Cutter received. He may be famous in the world of fly fishing, but in my book—and I hope in yours—he deserves to be punished.

"Let's consider the evidence, starting with Ms. Schlechter, the librarian. It's true neither she nor any other librarian actually saw Mr. Steele check out the copy of Mr. Cutter's book, but you'll remember Ms. Schlechter said the checkout system was designed to work that way, so that librarians would be left free to do other work. She also said there was less than a one percent chance that someone other than Mr. Steele could have checked out the book. The judge will shortly instruct you that you should base your verdict on a preponderance of the evidence"—she paused and watched while two or three jurors tried to cope with the word "preponderance," silently moving their lips as they did so—"that means there's more evidence supporting one side of the question than there is on the other. In this case, the preponderance is 99 percent in support of the conclusion that Mr. Steele checked out the book, which means you should accept that conclusion. And that proves he had access to the book, as the law requires to establish plagiarism.

"You'll recall Martin Kohl's testimony and the visual evidence showing the many instances in which Mr. Steele wantonly copied or nearly duplicated Mr. Cutter's words, which should establish beyond doubt in your minds that Steele acted with reckless disregard for Mr. Cutter's rights.

"Then there was Mr. Cutter's testimony that two years after his book was published, the Whiskey Creek Run in the Biscuit was destroyed by a flood and hasn't been worth fishing since. Yet Mr. Steele's book described Whiskey Creek Run in almost all the same words Mr. Cutter used, as if the run still existed two years *after* it was destroyed. You could not ask for more conclusive proof that Mr. Steele spent very little time or effort supposedly researching his book or he would have learned what happened at Whisky Creek. And you couldn't ask for more conclusive proof that he copied Mr. Cutter's work. That's not 'fair use,' as Mr. Bryce contended; that's plagiarism.

"Lars Lofgren, Mr. Cutter's publisher, testified that sales of Mr. Cutter's book took an unexpected nosedive after Mr. Steele's book was published. The decline was unexpected, because it did not follow the sales history of similar books Mr. Lofgren published. According to him, under a normal sales pattern the second printing of Mr. Cutter's book eventually would have sold out. The only reason he could think of for the sudden nosedive in sales was publication of

Mr. Steele's book, and he calculated that it cost Mr. Cutter $1,810 in royalties. Admittedly, $1,810 is not a great deal of money, but if, like Mr. Cutter, you're living on a pension and Social Security, as some of you may be, it seems like a lot, especially if it's money you earned through your own work, which Mr. Steele copied for his own benefit.

"Now let's look at the testimony of Trevor Dillon, who has spent much of his professional life studying cases like this. His comparative analysis of Mr. Cutter's and Mr. Steele's book showed Mr. Steele copied Mr. Cutter's words 47.2 percent of the time—almost half. He also testified that after extensive research he was unable to find any source of information giving the names and order of the Biscuit River pools other than Cutter's book, yet Mr. Steele's book recited the same list of pools by the same names and in the same order, further evidence that Mr. Steele copied Mr. Cutter's work. And I would remind you that Mr. Cutter accumulated his knowledge of the river over nearly an entire lifetime, while the only evidence we have is that Mr. Steele spent two days on the scene.

"When Mr. Bryce asked Mr. Dillon if the doctrine of fair use applies to this case, Mr. Dillon pointed out that it does not because Mr. Steele used nearly half of Mr. Cutter's words, which exceeds any reasonable definition of fair use. Despite Mr. Fairburn's opinion to the contrary, there's no way that much duplication of Mr. Cutter's work constitutes fair use.

"So let's review the facts. There's overwhelming evidence Mr. Steele had possession of Mr. Cutter's book for two months, more than enough time for him to copy everything he wanted from it. There is evidence Mr. Steele spent only two days in Wetside supposedly doing 'research' for his chapter on the Biscuit; there is no evidence he spent any more time than that. Mr. Cutter, by contrast, has spent most of his life on the river. You saw on the screen in this courtroom the unmistakable evidence that Mr. Steele copied huge portions of Mr. Cutter's work—47.2 percent, by Mr. Dillon's calculation. You heard testimony that Mr. Steele repeated almost word for word the description of

Whiskey Creek Run in Mr. Cutter's book—two years *after* Whiskey Creek Run was destroyed in a flood. You heard Mr. Lofgren describe what happened to the sales of Mr. Cutter's book—and his royalties—after Mr. Steele's book was published. You also heard testimony that Mr. Steele repeated Mr. Cutter's list of Biscuit River pools, a list not available anywhere else.

"All these facts, all the testimony and evidence, lead inescapably to the conclusion that Mr. Steele committed an outrageous, wanton, aggravated act of plagiarism, stealing Mr. Cutter's words and using them for his own financial benefit, forcing Mr. Cutter to bring suit against him. The facts and circumstances of this case lead to no other conclusion. Now you have the opportunity to punish Mr. Steele for his arrogant behavior, to punish him and assure he doesn't do this again. You can do that by returning a verdict that Mr. Cutter is entitled to actual damages for lost royalties and punitive damages in the full amount authorized by the law, $250,000. I urge you to look into your consciences and do so. Thank you."

I'd been watching Steele throughout Pine's summation, but his face remained impassive and his eyes downcast, giving the impression his mind was somewhere far away. He probably wished the rest of him was somewhere far away, too.

After Pine returned to her seat the judge asked Merritt Bryce if he was ready.

"Yes, Your Honor." He had again donned his pinstriped suit for the occasion and was wearing a red tie with a pattern of what looked like small dark hourglasses. He took his usual stance before the jury, cleared his throat, wiped his forehead, and began speaking.

"Ladies and gentlemen, I'm here this morning to convince you that this is *not* a case of plagiarism. Whatever similarities or duplications may exist between Mr. Cutter's book and Mr. Steele's chapter about the Biscuit River are the results either of coincidence or the fair use of copyrighted material. Despite what Ms. Pine says, there is nothing in the testimony and evidence you have seen and heard that proves conclusively that Mr. Steele's book harmed the sale of Mr. Cutter's book or injured him financially. And since there is no proof of actual damages to Mr. Cutter, it follows there cannot be any punitive damages, because Mr. Steele did nothing wrong.

"Let's review the evidence that leads to this conclusion, starting with the testimony of the librarian, Ms. Schlechter. As Ms. Pine conceded, she never actually saw the person who checked out Cutter's book from the library. She also did not know who renewed the book, or how. All she knew is that it was checked out on Steele's library card, but she admitted it was possible someone else could have used his card and she would have no way of knowing. Thus there is no provable evidence that Mr. Steele ever had the book in his possession, and under Oregon law the plaintiff must prove that he did have access to the book in order to win a judgment of plagiarism. That alone is sufficient for you to find that Mr. Steele is not at fault in this case.

"Now let's turn to Martin Kohl's testimony. Mr. Kohl, who had two years of community college without a single English class, who admitted he doesn't have time to read many books, and who has no other apparent literary or legal qualifications, nevertheless took it upon himself to find what he thought were similarities between Mr. Cutter's book and Mr. Steele's. Based on his total lack of qualifications to make such a judgment, I think you can disregard Mr. Kohl's testimony as being unworthy of consideration.

"Next we come to Mr. Bosenko's testimony. His records show Mr. Steele stayed at the Spruce Grove Motel two nights during the period he was doing research for his chapter on the Biscuit River. But Mr. Bosenko said he didn't know whether Mr. Steele might also have stayed at one or more of the Forest Service campgrounds in the area, and admitted Mr. Steele could have stayed in those campgrounds for six weeks or longer and he would never have known it. So Mr. Bosenko's testimony, like Ms. Schleicher's, is essentially worthless. It proves nothing.

"As for the testimony of Mr. Cutter, the plaintiff, he admitted it was his friend Martin Kohl who first suggested to him there might be similarities between his book and Mr. Steele's; it was never Mr. Cutter's idea. He also testified his publisher studied the matter and advised him not to file suit because the amount of money involved was so small it wasn't worth the trouble or expense. Mr. Cutter said he filed suit anyway because he was angry. I ask you, ladies and gentlemen, is that a good or valid reason for filing a lawsuit? For interrupting your work and your daily lives to drag you here for nearly a week to let Mr. Cutter vent his anger? I think you'll agree it is not.

"Lars Lofgren, Mr. Cutter's publisher, testified the unsold copies of the second printing of his book would have brought royalties of $1,810 if they had all been sold. Based on his testimony, that's the maximum amount Mr. Cutter could have expected to receive if every copy of the second printing had sold. But there's no evidence or testimony even suggesting the likelihood of that. The truth is that very few books sell out completely, regardless of circumstances; that's why publishers and bookstores have remainder sales. And neither Mr. Lofgren nor Mr. Cutter nor anyone else testified that publication of Mr. Steele's book actually hurt sales of Mr. Cutter's; Mr. Lofgren said merely that sales of Cutter's book didn't follow the same pattern as other fishing books he'd published. The truth is there's no evidence Steele's book impeded the sales of Mr. Cutter's book.

"Now let's consider the testimony of Trevor Dillon, Mr. Cutter's so-called expert. He admitted there are only a limited number of words in the English language that can be used to describe rivers or fish and fishing, so it's not surprising both Cutter and Steele used the same words; what would be surprising is if they hadn't. That was affirmed by the testimony of Peter Fairburn, our expert witness. Mr. Fairburn also testified that any other similarities or duplications fell under the doctrine of fair use and said categorically there was no plagiarism in this case.

"So if you consider all these facts, as I earnestly hope you will, you can come only to the conclusion there was no plagiarism, no financial harm to Mr. Cutter, no aggravated misconduct or disregard of Mr. Cutter's rights, and therefore no actual or punitive damages. But I would also ask you to keep in mind that Mr. Steele's life's work, his reputation and his livelihood are all on the line here and will inevitably suffer even if you find him free of liability. Just the publicity of having been dragged into this unnecessary lawsuit will assure that, and we have a reporter from a national magazine right here in the courtroom." He nodded in my direction, and the jurors all looked at me curiously.

Ouch! So much for anonymity.

"So," Bryce continued, "if there's any injured party in this case, it's Clint Steele. But you can minimize the harm by finding that he did nothing wrong. On his behalf, and mine, I sincerely urge you to do so. Thank you." He took an extra moment to look each juror in the eye, then returned to his seat.

I thought it was a pretty good argument.

Judge Frost asked Pine if she had any rebuttal and she responded affirmatively. She faced the jury and began pacing back and forth again. "Ladies and gentlemen, despite Mr. Bryce's conspiracy theory that someone other than Clint Steele might have checked Mickey Cutter's book out of the library, I would remind you of Mrs. Schlechter's testimony there's a less than one percent chance that could have happened. And absolutely no evidence that it did.

"Mr. Bryce also said you should disregard Martin Kohl's testimony because he didn't have any English classes in college, is not an avid reader, and therefore isn't qualified to judge whether Mr. Steele copied Mr. Cutter's words. I wonder how many of you never took a college English class? And what does it matter anyway? I think all of you can read, just as Martin Kohl can, and that's all that was necessary to determine there were duplications or similarities between Cutter's book and Steele's. You heard Mr. Kohl's testimony and saw for yourselves the slides with side-by-side comparisons of the two books. Those slides showed clearly that Mr. Steele copied many of Mr. Cutter's words, and I think you are all more than qualified to judge the truth of that.

"Mr. Bryce also told you to ignore Mr. Bosenko's testimony because he didn't know whether Mr. Steele might have stayed in one of several local campgrounds while he was purportedly doing 'research' on his book. Nobody else knows, either. The only evidence you have in front of you is that Mr. Steele spent two days at the Spruce Grove motel while supposedly 'researching' his chapter about fishing the Biscuit. There is not a shred of evidence or testimony he spent any more time. Your duty as jurors is to consider only the evidence you have seen and heard, so you should not consider any unsupported suppositions or suggestions to the contrary.

"Now I'd like to remind you of what Mr. Cutter had to say about what happened to Whiskey Creek Run. This might have been the most critical testimony in the trial, and Mr. Bryce, as you may have noticed, did not even mention it. That's because it proves that Mr. Steele copied Mr. Cutter's words, even though his description of Whiskey Creek Run was long out of date when he did so.

"As for Mr. Cutter himself, he testified he filed suit against Steele because he was angry. What's wrong with that? Wouldn't you be angry, too, if someone had stolen your work and used it for his own financial gain? Mr. Steele, as I said, is not charged with a crime, so the only means Mr. Cutter has of seeking retribution under the law is by filing a suit seeking damages. I suspect, under similar circumstances, most or all of you would do exactly the same thing. As for Mr. Steele, if this trial should happen to damage his reputation, that's not your worry; he has only himself to blame.

"As jurors you must rely only on the testimony and evidence you have heard and seen. If you do that, I believe you will come to the inescapable conclusion that Mr. Steele's theft of Mr. Cutter's words caused actual financial loss to Mr. Cutter and that Mr. Steele's outrageous actions should be punished by punitive damages." She looked the jurors in the eye one more time and sat down.

After a brief recess, the judge gaveled things back to order and told the jurors to listen carefully while he read the instructions he and the attorneys had formulated. Listening to a judge read jury instructions is even more tedious and boring than listening to voir dire questioning of jurors, so I basically tuned out while Judge Frost droned on. I perked up to listen only when he was describing the verdict form, which included a list of questions for the jurors to answer with their findings. Judging from their facial expressions, this made some of the jurors uncomfortable.

It was 11:14 when the judge finished and the bailiff led the jurors into the jury room, closed the door and left them to deliberate. I took out my paperback and settled down to read; I didn't want to leave the courtroom and possibly miss the verdict.

Nothing happened until about 12:30, when the bailiff went to the jury room, knocked, and told the jurors it was time for lunch, he was taking orders and would bring them whatever they ordered from the Riverside. Meanwhile, they could continue deliberating. I'd anticipated something like that might happen, so I'd brought a couple of candy bars.

The bailiff left with the orders and the attorneys, plaintiff, and defendant followed suit. The bailiff returned with a second deputy, each carrying a stack of Styrofoam containers, presumably the last free lunch the jurors would receive from Fremont County. Olivia Pine, Mickey Cutter, and Martin Kohl returned separately from the Riverside followed by Clint Steele and his attorneys. Everybody settled down and resumed waiting.

At 2:49 p.m., there was a loud knock on the jury room door. The bailiff answered, nodded, turned in our direction to say, "we have a verdict," then headed for the judge's chambers to let him know.

When all the players were reassembled in the courtroom and the clerk and court reporter had materialized from somewhere, Judge

Frost ordered the bailiff to bring in the jury. They seated themselves noisily in the box and the judge asked if they had reached a verdict. The retired forest ranger stood—I was glad to see they had elected him foreman—and said, "yes we have, Your Honor." He handed the verdict form to the clerk, who passed it to the judge. He scanned it, handed it back to the clerk and asked her to read it. She cleared her throat and in a high-pitched voice read: "Fremont County Case number CA2306, Cutter versus Steele. We, the jurors in the above-entitled case, answer the questions posed by the court as follows:

"Question 1: Has the plaintiff proven the elements necessary to recover actual damages? Answer: Yes.

"Question 2: Should actual damages be awarded against the defendant? Answer: Yes.

"Question 3: If the answer to Question 2 is yes, what amount of actual damages should be awarded against the defendant? Answer: $1,810.

"Question 4: Has the plaintiff proven the elements necessary to recover punitive damages? Answer: Yes.

"Question 5: If the answer to Question 4 is yes, what amount of punitive damages should be awarded against the defendant? Answer: $245,000."

Clint Steele stared at the floor while the verdict was read. After the final question was answered, he stood and walked swiftly with long, determined strides up the aisle and out of the courtroom, leaving his lawyers looking after him in surprise. By then Mickey Cutter also was on his feet, awkwardly hugging Olivia Pine, and Martin Kohl soon joined in a group hug.

Meanwhile I banged away on my laptop, trying to capture everything I'd heard and seen before I forgot it. The courtroom was nearly empty by the time I finished; only Pine and Kohl remained, conversing at the plaintiff's table until Kohl looked up and headed in my direction.

"Mr. Kane," he started to say, but I interrupted.

"How do you know my name?"

He looked surprised. "Oh, everybody knows who you are. Look, Mickey had to leave to let his wife know what happened, but he asked me to tell you he and his wife are hosting a little victory celebration this evening and he would like it very much if you can attend. Ms. Pine and I will be there, too. Mickey's wife is a great cook, and I imagine you're about ready for some home cooking after eating at the Riverside all week."

He was right about that. It also would give me a chance to talk with Mickey Cutter, which I needed to do. I wanted to talk to Steele, too—if he was willing to talk—but thought I might catch up with him at the Spruce Grove. I thanked Kohl and told him I'd be delighted to come.

"Great. I'm going to pick up Olivia at the motel at four o'clock. I can give you a ride, too, if that works." I assured him it would, and we all left the courtroom together.

On the way back to the motel I stopped at Mike's Market in hopes of buying some flowers to take to Mrs. Cutter. They had none, so I decided to get a bottle of wine instead. The selection was small, with only a few of Oregon's famous Willamette Valley pinot noirs on the shelf, but I chose the most expensive—$19.95—figuring I'd put it on my expense account.

Steele's SUV was missing from the parking lot when I reached the motel. Bosenko, sitting grumpily behind his counter, verified the great fly fisher had hurriedly checked out. "The sumbitch was here five nights and paid for only four 'cause of that mouse he let loose," he said.

"Don't feel bad. He just got nicked by the jury for nearly a quarter-million dollars."

"Hah! Good! Serves him right."

But I was disappointed at having missed Steele. Now I'd have to try somehow to reach him by phone.

At four o'clock I went downstairs and found Olivia Pine sheltering from the rain beneath the drive-through canopy. I offered her congratulations and asked if she knew why the jury had brought in a punitive verdict of $245,000 instead of the maximum. "Who knows?" she said. "Juries do funny things. And that was a pretty strange jury."

Just then Kohl's SUV entered the parking lot with a crunch of gravel. I opened the passenger door to let Pine get in, then got in the back seat. Kohl turned around and drove through Wetside, heading west out of town. "Mickey's place is about six miles from here, so it won't take long," he said.

On the way we chatted amiably about the trial, and I dodged several questions about what I intended to write and how I intended to write it. Then everyone fell silent because something strange had just happened: The rain had stopped. The sky was still ominous and threatening but for the moment at least there were no new drops on the windshield.

We drove on through dripping woods with occasional glimpses of the Biscuit River through the foliage on our left until we came to a cleared spot with a wide pull-off overlooking the river. A single vehicle was parked in the pull-off. Then I did a double take; the vehicle had a brightly colored decal of a leaping trout on its side. "Hey," I said. "That's Clint Steele's car."

"Really?" Kohl said. "Wonder what he's doing here? Let's go find out." He slowed, made a U-turn in the middle of the empty highway, and headed back, gesturing toward the pull-off. "This is the Gravy Pool," he said. "You know, biscuits and gravy. Get it?"

Yeah, I got it.

"It's one of the best pools in the river, but I doubt there's any steelhead here now. Anyway, I'd like to see Steele fish." He drove into the puddled pull-off and parked next to Steele's Suburban, which was unoccupied. We all got out and walked to the edge of the pull-off, which dropped off steeply about twenty-five or thirty feet down to the river.

Kohl got there first, peered over the edge for a moment, then swore out loud, turned and started running back to his SUV. Wondering what he'd seen, I looked over the edge. The Biscuit's water was shivering in a breeze, but then the breeze passed, the water flattened and at the downstream end of the pool I made out a pair of black waders submerged in three or four feet of water. Then I realized a man was wearing the waders, lying facedown on the river's rocky bottom. Olivia Pine gasped when she saw where I was pointing.

Kohl returned, pulling on a pair of his own waders he'd fetched from the back of his SUV. "Call 911," he told Pine, then started down a steep, rain-slippery trail toward the river. I started to follow, but the going was tricky and uncertain, forcing me to dig in my heels or grasp roots protruding here and there from the face of the cliff. Kohl practically slid the whole way down and was already in the river by the time I reached the bottom. He managed to secure a grip on the back of the prostrate man's black waders and started dragging him toward shore while I discarded my shoes and socks, rolled up my pants and waded in to help.

The waders were full of water, which made their occupant hard to move, but together we got him ashore. There was no doubt it was Clint Steele; the neat little hair bun on the back of his head was a giveaway. Kohl rolled him onto his side, thumped him on the back several times and we watched water drain from his slack mouth. Kohl knelt, felt for a pulse and shook his head, then turned Steele onto his back, straddled him and began CPR. I watched, feeling helpless, until Kohl grew tired and said, "your turn." I took his place and tried duplicating his movements while he checked again for a pulse and once more shook his head. We kept taking turns until finally Kohl said, "I think it's useless."

Just then we heard the "whoop-whoop" of an arriving emergency vehicle, and in another minute a sheriff's deputy was scrambling down the trail to join us. Without a word, he tried taking Steele's pulse, then peeled back the great fly fisher's eyelids and found the pupils fixed and dilated. "He's gone," the deputy said. Half-rolling the body over, he reached in Steele's hip pocket and removed his wallet, then fished his car keys out of a front pocket and handed them to me. "Take these up to the sheriff," he said, pointing at the top of the bank. "He told me to wait here for the firefighters or the coroner, but he wants these."

I pocketed the wallet and keys and started climbing back up to the pull-off. Going up was even harder than coming down, but this time Kohl had more trouble than I did because he was still wearing waders, so I reached the top first. Olivia Pine was waiting with a stern-faced uniformed man with white hair and a white handlebar mustache. He stepped forward with hand extended and said, "I'm Sheriff Lafayette Abercrombie." I started to introduce myself, but he said "I know who you are. Everybody does."

I gave him the wallet and keys and Abercrombie checked the identification in the wallet, nodded and said, "Let's have a look at his vehicle."

We all walked over to the Suburban—Kohl had joined us by this time—and looked through the driver's-side window, where we saw a sheet of paper bearing a brief handwritten note on the seat. Abercrombie unlocked the door, produced a latex glove from a pocket, put it on, reached inside, and picked up the paper, turning it over as he did so. That's when I saw the note was written on the back side of one of Steele's $25 autographed photos.

Abercrombie read the note aloud: "'There is no refuge from confession but suicide; and suicide is confession.' It's signed by Clint Steele." He held out the note so everyone could see it.

Kohl looked puzzled. "I don't get it," he said.

"Wait a minute," I said. "I think I recognize that." I read it again. "Yeah, I do know it. It's a famous quote from a court argument by Daniel Webster."

"But what does it mean?" Kohl asked.

"It means Clint Steele just wrote the end of my story for me."

"How so?"

"He plagiarized his own suicide note."

THE FIRST WORDS EVER
WRITTEN ABOUT FLY FISHING

I have heard of a Macedonian way of catching fish and it is this . . . They fasten red wool around a hook, and fix onto the wool two feathers which grow under a cock's wattles, and which in color are like wax. Their rod is six feet long, and their line is the same length. Then they throw their snare and the fish, attracted and maddened by the color, comes straight at it thinking from the pretty sight to gain a dainty mouthful; when, however, it opens its jaws, it is caught by the hook, and enjoys a bitter repast, a captive.
                    —Claudius Aelianus, circa AD 175–235

ON THE XVIIth of the month, as was their custom, members of the Anglers Club of Rome assembled for their regular monthly meeting. Dressed in togas, they seated themselves on benches in two concentric rings facing a stone platform where guest speakers traditionally held forth. Some sipped wine and soon began snoring softly. Others munched grapes or olives, spitting seeds and pits on the stone floor.

Marcus Severus, the club president, opened the meeting as usual by asking for fishing reports. Gluteus Maximus, one of the club's oldest, fattest, most esteemed members, who was known for always sitting down while he fished, struggled to his feet. He smoothed his toga, looked around, and began to speak, reporting he had fished the Nera, a tributary of the Tiber, on the XIIIth. "I caught two fish, which I tempted with the nether parts of a roasting fowl," he said. "The fish consumed this bait with alacrity. What the fish are called I know not, but they were exceeding ugly and did not struggle much. I offered them as food to my servants, which they declined."

Then stood Septimus Publius, who said he had fished for wrasse along the rocky shoreline of a small bay in the Tyrrhenian Sea on the VIIth. "Upon the beach I found the reeking remains of a dead crab," he reported. "Since the wrasse, as you know, is an eater of meat, I decided to use a portion of the crab for bait. I shooed away several gulls that were feeding upon it, fixed what was left upon my hook and lobbed it as far as possible into the sea. The bait was seized almost immediately by a fish, a wrasse of such splendid size and color that I quickly decided to keep it. I presented it to my dear wife, who cleaved it in half and cooked it with pasta. We ate equal portions, so I suppose you could say we each enjoyed a half-wrassed dinner."

He sat down amid a chorus of groans from his fellow members. Some pelted him with olive pits.

For a time no one else stood to report. Then old Sextus Aolus rose awkwardly, cleared his throat, and admitted that on the XIVth he had taken a skunking on the main stem of the Tiber. "Though it was not a wasted occasion, far from it," he added. "From my vantage point I had the pleasure to observe a fair young maiden descend the bank to the river and, insensible as she was to my presence, disrobe entirely and bathe, to my considerable delight."

This was greeted by hoots and catcalls by other members.

When the hubbub subsided and it was obvious no further fishing reports were forthcoming, Marcus Severus introduced the night's guest speaker, Leonidas Wulfiviius, a well-traveled angler of some renown. He had been invited to tell about a recent fishing trip to Macedonia, a distant land no one else in the room had ever visited.

With dramatic gestures, Wulfiviius described how his Macedonian hosts had taken him to a river where local anglers had cleverly fashioned lures by winding bits of red wool around the shaft of a hook, then adding a pair of "wax-colored" feathers "which grow under a cock's wattles." This feathered creation, he said, was attached to the end of a braided hair line which in turn was affixed to the end of a short wooden pole or rod. The angler then used the rod to dap the feathered lure on the river's surface, where fine, speckled, streamlined fish would sometimes rise clear out of the water and take the offering.

"It was a deadly method," Leonidas said. "I witnessed them catch great baskets of fish. They invited me to try and I was amazed at how easy it was to catch the fish—and how much fun!"

One member asked Wulfiviius where a cock's wattles were located, but he ignored the question. Another asked the name of the river he had fished. "They told me it was called the Astræus," Wulfiviius replied, "but I think they made up the name to keep me from learning the true one. Those Macedonians treat us Romans with great suspicion, perhaps with some justification."

The Anglers Club members who were still awake listened carefully to all this, but one among them, a youthful scribe, listened more intently than all the rest, apparently growing more excited at every word of Wulfiviius' discourse. When the speaker had finished, the scribe, whose name was Claudius Aelianus—everybody called him Al for short—did not even stay for the raffle. Instead, he rushed from the chamber and ran through the dark streets to his room and lit a candle. As its flickering flame cast great dancing shadows on the bare walls, he brushed aside a stack of parchment scrolls containing the unfinished work that had occupied his time for many months, his *De Natura Animalium* ("On the Nature of Animals"). He took up a fresh scroll, smoothed it on his worktable, tacked down the corners, picked up a stylus and dipped it in ink, anxious to begin writing while Leonidas Wulfiviius's words were still fresh in his mind.

Then he stopped for a moment to think about exactly what he was going to say. Leonidas Wulfiviius' report was important and exciting; he had actually *been there* and seen the Macedonians fishing, had even tried it himself. That was about as trustworthy as information could be, much better than some of the second-, third-, fourth- or fifth-hand accounts Aelianus had unearthed from ancient scrolls in various libraries and included in his work—a necessity, because he had hardly ever been anywhere or seen anything himself. Yet he remained troubled about the accuracy of some of those library accounts—could it really be true that goats breathed through their ears, or that beaver ate their own testicles? That's what he'd found in the libraries, so that's what he'd written about them, though it seemed unlikely.

Leonidas' report, by contrast, was about as close to the truth as you could get without actually being there. Still, Aelianus thought, it might be a good idea to qualify Leonidas' account just a bit and admit he had not actually been an eyewitness or participant.

Having made that decision, he leaned over the fresh scroll and started writing, beginning with these words:

"I have heard of a Macedonian way of catching fish and it is this . . ."

And the rest, as they say, is history.

ACKNOWLEDGMENTS

THIS BOOK is dedicated to my dear wife, Joan Zimmerman Raymond. Her devotion and sacrifice have made possible my fishing and writing lives, and so much more. Somehow she has managed to put up with me for nearly sixty years, and if you have gleaned any pleasure or insight from these pages, or any of my other books, you owe her just as I do.

I've been fortunate to have many great fishing partners, but none better than my son Randy—no genetic manipulation necessary. His companionship and assistance contributed more to this book than he knows. Thanks for everything, Randy.

Dave Draheim is another fishing partner, though I can't remember we caught very many fish together. He supported his fishing habit by working as an attorney and deserves my special thanks for graciously reading a preliminary draft of "The Man in Black Waders" and guiding me through the thickets of courtroom procedure. I didn't accept all his good advice, however; it would have made an already long story even longer.

The dust jacket painting on this book is the work of my good long-distance friend Al Hassall, whose art I have always admired.

Finally, grateful thanks to another long-distance friend, Paul Schullery, for his understanding, wisdom, and support.

ABOUT THE AUTHOR

STEVE RAYMOND, a native of Bellingham, Washington, had a thirty-year career as a reporter, editor and manager at the Seattle *Times*. He also edited two magazines, *The Flyfisher* and *Fly Fishing in Salt Waters*, and reviewed fishing books for several publications. A charter and honorary life member of the Federation of Fly Fishers (now called Fly Fishing International), he is author of a dozen fly-fishing books, including two award-winning classics, *The Year of the Angler* and *The Year of the Trout*. His other titles include *Steelhead Country, The Estuary Flyfisher, Rivers of the Heart, Blue Upright, Nervous Water* and *Trout Quintet*. He received the prestigious Roderick Haig-Brown Award for significant contributions to angling literature and his work has appeared in nine anthologies and at least twenty-four magazines. His manuscripts and papers are now part of special collections at the Western Washington University libraries in Bellingham. In October 2022 he was admitted to the Fly Fishing Hall of Fame.

Raymond and his wife, Joan, reside on an old farm on Whidbey Island in northern Puget Sound. He can be reached at steveraymondbooks@whidbey.com.